QUESTIONS TO GROW BY

10/23/04

To Barbara Featherston
daughter of dear friend Kay Tipp,
with warmest greetings & best wishes.

Ken Helfant

QUESTIONS TO GROW BY

♦

A Path to Emotional Maturity

Ken Helfant

iUniverse, Inc.
New York Lincoln Shanghai

QUESTIONS TO GROW BY
A Path to Emotional Maturity

Copyright © 2005 by Kenneth G. Helfant

All rights reserved. No part of this book may be used or reproduced by any means, graphic, electronic, or mechanical, including photocopying, recording, taping or by any information storage retrieval system without the written permission of the publisher except in the case of brief quotations embodied in critical articles and reviews.

iUniverse books may be ordered through booksellers or by contacting:

iUniverse
2021 Pine Lake Road, Suite 100
Lincoln, NE 68512
www.iuniverse.com
1-800-Authors (1-800-288-4677)

Cover design by Bruce Gourley, Oceano, CA

ISBN-13: 978-0-595-36696-5 (pbk)
ISBN-13: 978-0-595-81119-9 (ebk)
ISBN-10: 0-595-36696-1 (pbk)
ISBN-10: 0-595-81119-1 (ebk)

Printed in the United States of America

This book is dedicated to Douglas Helfant,
Cynthia Helfant-Turner, Hilary Helfant-Youngerman,
Alex & Matthew Helfant-Calderon, Ward & Grace Turner-Helfant,
& Milo Youngerman-Helfant

Contents

Preface ix
Introduction 1

Part I   *Your Early History* 9
ONE. WHERE DID YOU COME FROM? 13
TWO. YOUR CHILDHOOD AND ADOLESCENCE: WHAT
WAS GOOD, WHAT WAS BAD? 28

Part II   *Challenges to Attaining Emotional Maturity* . 41
THREE. HOW DO YOU HANDLE ANGER, FEAR,
SADNESS? 43
FOUR. HOW DO YOU HANDLE DISTURBING FACTS AND
FEELINGS? 57
FIVE. HOW'S YOUR LOVE AND SEX LIFE? 75

Part III   *How Emotionally Mature Are You?* 93
SIX. WHO ARE YOU? 97

Part IV   *Your Future: The World's Future* 115
SEVEN. WHO DO YOU WANT TO BECOME? 117
Epilogue 135

Bibliography 137
Acknowledgments 141

Preface

In preparing to write this book, I read all the psychology self-help books I could get my hands on. I didn't find one that I am in serious disagreement with. I found the differences between them are usually matters of emphasis. They all give good advice in the areas they emphasize. The essential question is whether the areas they emphasize relates to what you need.

It is estimated that there are over four hundred "schools" of psychotherapy in the U.S.. Though most of them rely principally on psychology, almost all incorporate insights from other fields as well. A good example are the masterful books of Thomas Moore, which combine insights from spirituality, philosophy, and psychology.

When I first became a psychotherapist I was most strongly influenced by Harry Stack Sullivan, and. for several years, considered myself an interpersonal psychologist. From there I progressed, in a series of stages, to where I presently find myself: most strongly influenced by Michael White and David Epston (Narrative Therapy), Ken Wilbur (Integral Psychology), and Marshall Rosenberg (Non-Violent Communication).

Although my central focus has changed several times in the course of my career, I am still influenced, when I believe it is appropriate, by aspects of my earlier central foci.

I believe we should let every flower bloom. I also believe that readers should decide which flower is best for them. To aid you in deciding if this book is likely to be best for you, here is a very condensed summary of it:

QUESTIONS TO GROW BY presents seven Central Questions in developmental order. Responding to the Seven Central Questions and the exercises accompanying each of them helps you to become more fully aware of your life story and how and why it developed as it has. It may reveal that you are fixated, to some degree, on a level of psychological development that is less than you are capable of. It goes on to help you become your own psychotherapist and make revisions in your life story and conduct which will allow you to attain a more satisfying level of emotional maturity.

Introduction

○ ○

*We can all help ourselves to change, to grow,
to become the person it is in us to be.
We can learn to be our own best friend.*

—*Mildred Newman & Bernard Berkowitz*

When Marine Architects wish to denote the spot on a sail which, if the wind were concentrated on the spot, it would have the same effect as it does when it is spread over the sail, they draw a cross through, and double circles around, that spot:

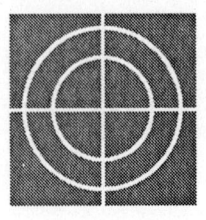

It is called the "center of effort." This nautical symbol is the inspiration for my personal logo:

It symbolizes my wish to have my center of effort come from my heart. Marshall Rosenberg uses a giraffe as his personal logo. Giraffes have the largest hearts of any animal. In different ways we are both symbolizing our wish to come from our hearts and encourage others to come from their hearts. He has concentrated his efforts on the development of nonviolent communication (NVC). I have concentrated my efforts on the encouragement of individual growth by means of growth-inducing questions (GIQ).

I am eighty three years old. I have undoubtedly grown old, but I cannot say that I am fully grown up. What I can say is "I am working at it, and making better progress than ever." After trying many paths, I have found the path that works best for me is asking myself questions to check the maturity of my behavior and emotional responses, followed by working on changing those that I consider immature. In the course of doing this I have developed seven primary questions and an average of six helping questions for each of the primary questions.

I have used, and continue to use, my personal selections from this list of questions to help me grow in emotional maturity. Here is a summary of how it worked for me, as I hope it will work for you:

My parents were divorced when I was seven years old. At that time I didn't have any idea what divorce meant. All I knew was that my parents disappeared and my sister and I began living with another couple who acted like them, but in a more detached way. A week later my uncle (my father's brother} took us to New York City, put us on a train, an told us that the next day the train would leave us off in Chicago, where my father would be waiting for us. We were met in Chicago by my father and the woman he was living with. We lived with them for two years after which my mother (whom I didn't recognize at the time) suddenly appeared with a police officer and her new husband. Her new husband drove us all to Cliffside Park, New Jersey, a suburb of New York City. My sister and I lived in Cliffside Park with my mother, stepfather. and foster brother until I left for college.

At age fifty-seven, a practicing psychotherapist with three children, I found myself in the same position my father was in when I was seven years old—being divorced by my wife. I was deeply depressed. I began to explore my life in detail, trying to determine how and why this had happened to me. I knew that it had something to do with my early experiences in life, and began to explore those experiences in detail. These explorations resulted in Central Questions One and Two of QUESTIONS TO GROW BY: Where Did You Come From? and What Was Good, What Was Bad About Your Childhood? Probing my childhood with the help of these two questions caused me to realize that my childhood experiences left me with a deep feeling that I had no control, or even influence, over what happened to me. In discussions with my college roommate I first expressed my belief that I was like a chip afloat on the ocean, carried to wherever the wind and waves happened to take me. I accepted this as a central theme of my life at that time and for many years thereafter.

Through responding to Central Questions One and Two and their accompanying "helping questions "I became aware that as a child, I actually was like a chip afloat on the ocean with no control over the direction I took. As a result I behaved in a detached manner, even in my closest relationships. As I probed my first responses and their consequences I gradually came to realize that I now have considerable power to direct my own life, but that I didn't fully exercise it. For the first time I became aware of my contribution to my wife's decision to divorce me. In the course of our marriage, I took a basically detached posture, which, in the course of years of individual, group, couple, and family therapy had been suggested to me several times, but its origin never explained. When I became aware of its origin I was able to adopt a new life story, that of William Ernest Henley, "I am the master of my fate, I am the captain of my soul."

As I lived by my new life-story my depression lifted. I took charge of my life, acknowledged my responsibilities without condemning myself, and resumed my emotional growth in areas where it had stopped because of immature reactions to some of the events of my earlier life.

It is likely that you have already asked yourself most, if not all, of the Seven Central Questions. It is unlikely, however, that you have asked them in developmental order. It is even more unlikely that you have asked yourself the "helping questions" that accompany each of the central questions.

Unearthing dark corners of your life may temporarily lead to more psychological dysfunction than is safe to handle without a therapist. This concern is legitimate. We all need support in facing serious emotional problems. Because of this, I highly recommend that you join with a trustworthy friend if you have any anxiety on this score, or with a psychotherapist if you do not have such a friend. I think you will find that almost all psychotherapists are agreeable to self-questioning. Using it with a narrative therapist will be especially effective, but using it with any form of psychotherapy is likely to increase the effectiveness of that therapy and decrease the time needed to achieve the desired results.

Though I can't guarantee that you won't feel uneasy at times as a result of looking into yourself, I can guarantee that after you do so, your self-esteem and personal happiness will increase. I urge you to always remain best friends with yourself. If you find yourself confronting aspects of yourself that you don't like, have faith in the fact that they can be changed: as your own best friend, you will be the agency through which they are changed.

If you were blessed with an ideally healthy emotional development and have no organic defect, you may have already developed into a fully conscious, emotionally mature adult with an appropriately healthy life script, and will have no need for this book. If, like most of us, you have not been so blessed, you are invited to overcome whatever developmental handicaps you discover. Careful and honest responses to the questions you select to focus on is essential, plus systematic practice of the suggested exercises or whatever you believe you must do to overcome any problem you discover. Achieving fuller awareness of yourself will help you adopt a new and healthier life script with the help of which you can improve, maintain, and surpass yourself. It is my hope that in addition to personal gain, you will also join with others who are interested in fuller self-awareness. With their help and awareness of the political, economic, and environmental crises our world confronts, you can help co-create a more emotionally mature society. The way human beings relate to each other and the planet could very well determine whether the human race will survive. QUESTIONS focuses on psychological development. It only touches on social, political, philosophical, and economic issues, which are certainly as important, sometimes more important, than psychological issues, in determining human survival. Nevertheless, keeping in mind that the good of the whole begins with the individual is additional justification for developing yourself as an individual.

You can start on Central Question One and systematically go through each of the Central Questions in turn; or you can select the Central Question that interests you most, go through that question, and then decide whether you want to go through any or all of the remaining questions.

Here is a list of all of the Central and Helping Questions:

Central Question One: Where Did You Come From?

    Helping Questions

        1.1 What do you know about your family of origin and how does it affect your feelings about yourself and others?

        1.2 How did you/do you react to your culture and subculture(s)?

        1.3 What was the first role you remember playing in your family of origin?

        1.4 What were your family's secrets and lies?

Central Question Two: Your Childhood and Adolescence: What Was Good, What Was Bad?

    Helping Questions

        2.1 What is your most significant childhood memory?

        2.2 What formal and informal roles did you play in your family of origin?

        2.3 Did your family live by the values they professed?

        2.4 Were your siblings your friends?

        2.5 Were your peers your friends?

Central Question Three: How Do You Handle Anger, Fear, Sadness?

Helping Questions

    3.1 Do you get mad instead of sad; forbear instead of share?

    3.2 What are you most afraid of and why?

    3.3 Do you cry at the movies?

    3.4 Are you tormented by guilt?

    3.5 Do you con yourself and others about what you feel?

    3.6 Who are your models for handling early emotions?

    3.7 Does humor play a role In your life?

    3.8 What makes you happiest?

Central Question Four: How Do You Handle Disturbing Facts and Feelings?

Helping Questions

    4.1 Are you a denier?

    4.2 What are you addicted to?

    4.3 Are you a blamer?

    4.4 Do you have psychosomatic symptoms?

    4.5 Are you a rigid role player?

    4.6 Are you an above-it-aller?

    4.7 Are you a disdainer?

    4.8 Are you a power seeker?

    4.9 Do your defenses interfere with your ability to love and be loved?

    4.10 Do your defenses sometimes cause you to violate you own beliefs?

Central Question Five: How's Your Love and Sex Life?

Helping Questions

    5.1 Are you a sucker for romance?

    5.2 What were your first, and what are your current sexual fantasies?

5.3 What, for you, Is the ideal relationship between love and sex?

5.4 What were the prescribed love and sex roles when you were growing up?

5.5 How, if at all, did falling In love change your concepts of love and sex?

5.6 How, if at all, do gender stereotypes affect the way you conduct yourself as a lover?

5.7 How is the mesh between your role and the role of your lover?

Central Question Six: Who Are You?

Helping Questions

6.1 What are your current life roles?

6.2 Are you comfortable with your current life roles?

6.3 Did you ever try to buy or steal love?

6.4 How did your relationships with peers affect your feelings of belonging?

6.5 Who stuck with who in your family of origin? Who did you trust? Who did you distrust?

6.6 What is the nature and quality of your involvement in social groups?

6.7 What is the nature and quality of your involvement in work groups?

6.8 How are you doing in your present family? Are there changes you want to make?

Central Question Seven: Who Do You Want To Become?

Helping Questions

7.1 Do your images of your future reveal a direction and goals which encourage further growth?

7.2 If much of your growth has been accidental or situational, how can you position yourself to grow intentionally?

7.3 Have you focused on a particular aspect of human culture and ignored some others such as the arts, philosophy, physical health?

> 7.4 Are there specific steps you can take to promote further growth in yourself?

In line with the principles of narrative therapy, this book does not give advice. It emphasizes finding and being your true self through asking yourself questions designed to enlarge your understanding of yourself. I recommend that you select the Central Question that interests you most and work on it as recommended. If that helps, you may decide to work on some more, possibly all, of the questions. I have worked on all of the questions, as have most of the people I use as examples, but there are some examples of people who used only one or two, which gave them all the help they needed.

Each Central Question deals with developmental problems associated with a particular stage of emotional growth. By responding to them, with the help of the helping questions that accompany each Central Question, you will learn important things about yourself and may elect to make appropriate revisions in your life script. But that in itself will be of limited value unless you act on what you learn. So you can get to know about yourself "in your bones," each question is followed by one or more action and/or reflective exercise.

As per Thich Nhat Hahn, "Once there is seeing, there must be acting. Otherwise, what is the use of seeing?"—doing the exercises is essential for changing your behavior. The "Extra Mile," which follows most of the exercises offers additional experience. The more Extra Miles you do the greater is your chance to grow emotionally in areas where you may have only grown older.

I strongly recommend that you join or organize a GROUP of two or more (the more the better) and respond to and discuss QUESTIONS together. I have found that those who form or join such groups are much more likely to follow through with responding to the Exercises and Extra Miles. Those who undertake QUESTIONS alone often wind up skipping these two important follow-throughs.

The people I describe in this book suffered from mild to severe emotional wounds. They all made progress in healing and subsequent emotional growth. They diminished interpersonal hostility in their lives and are now better equipped and better motivated to help their society do the same.

PART I

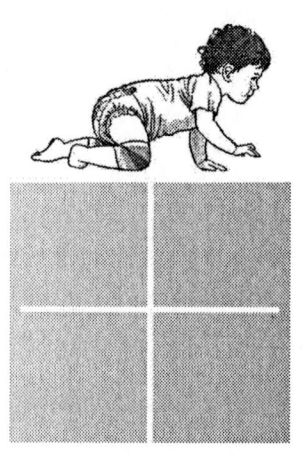

Your Early History

○ ○
Answering questions about yourself—the right questions—can help you to take a step back from the situation, to get honest with yourself, and to start thinking about your options.

—*Philip C. McGraw*

Part One, includes Central Questions One and Two. It focuses on your experiences before you were fully able to express yourself. Being unable to fully express yourself at the time you had these experiences makes them especially difficult to remember, but doesn't reduce their effects. The questions in Part One will help you remember them, assess their effect on you, and help you to modify these effects if you believe you should. Or, as Philip C. McGraw puts it, "Know your history so you can walk out of it."

As will be described in Helping Question 1.3, *What Were Your Family's Secrets and Lies?*, Tom learned from his mother that his father physically abused him when he was very young. This came as a shock to him, he had completely repressed any memory of it. When he became aware of it he was able to understand it and recover from its ill effects.

Marie was sexually abused as a child by her stepfather, but repressed all memory of it. This experience seriously affected her behavior as an adult, as will be described in her response to Helping Question 2.1, *Which Childhood Experiences Stimulated, Which Stunted, Your Emotional Growth?*

Tom and Marie's problems and their resolution express the essence of what QUESTIONS is about. If, at some point before you have attained emotional maturity in a particular area your emotional growth in that area is blocked, it is very difficult, in some cases impossible, to grow beyond that point. In Tom's case growth from fearful to cooperative relationships with authority was stopped. In Marie's case, growth from fear of sex to enjoyment of sex was stopped. Emotional growth in an area where normal growth has been stopped will continue only if and when such stoppage is resolved.

The basic technique used in QUESTIONS is an updated form of Socratic self-questioning. In Socrates' time (about 500 B.C.), the stages of human emotional development were not clearly understood, so his self-questioning was in random order. Since then a great deal of psychological and biological research has resulted in detailed knowledge of the stages in human development. QUESTIONS draws upon this research and presents questions stage by stage.

Each of the Central Questions with their accompanying Helping Questions constitutes a chapter. Each chapter helps you define any emotional handicaps you may have developed in the course of your experience with the developmental stage described in that chapter. It then goes on to recommend actions which will help you resolve any handicaps you may have discovered.

I strongly recommend that as you read this book you share your thoughts and feelings about any part of it that causes you to feel anxious with at least one person. It is difficult, and sometimes impossible, to define and resolve such anxiety without feedback from someone you trust and respect.

CENTRAL QUESTION ONE

WHERE DID YOU COME FROM?

o o o o o o o o o o o o o o o o o o o o o o o o o o o o o
*In the great game of life, one week we're spectators,
and the next week we're performers.*

—Garrison Keillor

During the summer of 1950 I taught social psychology at Hampton Institute in Virginia, an all-black college with a racially mixed faculty. I asked class members to choose a topic for their term papers from a list of titles that I thought would interest them. "The Roots of Racial Prejudice in the U.S.A." was among the titles I suggested. To my surprise, no one selected it. I asked why, certain that everyone in the class had feelings about it, and some probably had very strong feelings about it. The students told me that they didn't want to write about racial prejudice in the USA, because in order to do so, they would have to acknowledge that their ancestors were slaves I shouldn't have been surprised. Who likes to face painful facts?

By sharing some ideas which later evolved into QUESTIONS, I was able to convince my students that shunning their enslaved ancestry interfered with their truly knowing themselves. Outside their awareness, they had absorbed the very prejudice they fervently opposed! So much so, that they were ashamed of their own backgrounds! This is a dramatic example of how where one comes from (in this case from ancestors who were slaves and a society prejudiced against blacks), can result in thoughts, attitudes, and feelings that severely interfere with personal emotional growth.

If a plant's roots are ailing they can be strengthened by fertilizing, watering, and/or exposing the plant's leaves to more sunlight. If your roots are ailing—as my students' roots were—you can strengthen them by changing something in yourself or in your current physical or human environment that needs to be changed. Only by systematically examining yourself and your environment can you decide what needs to be altered. As with the students in my social psychology class, you may be acting on deeply-rooted destructive beliefs, even though you, yourself, are the victim.

Sensitized by the Civil Rights and Women's Rights movements, many of us have become aware of factors in our past that seriously impair our ability to see and experience ourselves and our environment clearly. Looking into your early relationships with members of other racial and ethnic groups in a systematic fashion, you may find personal beliefs and feelings that can and should be changed.

As Garrison Keillor points out, we start as observers, then become performers. Our initial performances are copies of what we observed and experienced from our parents, teachers, and other role models. If we don't attain insight into ourselves, later performances remain copies of behaviors learned in our early physical, cultural, social, emotional, and spiritual environments.

Some people become, and remain throughout their lives, exactly as their roots directed them to become and remain. Others become aware of roots that are life-enhancing, and roots that are not. This understanding enables them to alter their script if this is necessary for them to grow into the people they want to be. They perform according to the script they were brought up with only if, after carefully examining it, they find themselves in agreement with it.

Sample vignettes of experiences of various people who, with the help of QUESTIONS, went through this sequence are recorded after each helping question and accompanying exercises. All of the things described actually happened, but names, geographical locations, and other facts that might reveal actual identities have been changed (except for those relating to myself). Ongoing detailed backgrounds and responses to questions plus exercises will be given for me and for three of my former clients. These are my initial impressions of my three former clients:

> **Angelica:** "Tall, dark and beautiful" was a beauty-contest winner in her youth. She is spontaneous, loves to exhibit herself, doesn't hesitate to express her feelings, whether positive or negative. She had problems with two husbands, the second of whom persuaded her to enroll in a "Know Thyself" course which I conducted as part of the adult education program of the First Unitarian-Universalist Church of San Diego.
>
> **Anthony:** "Tall, dark and handsome" is a successful attorney. He plays tennis, tells jokes, and is well liked. The apparent ease with which he has mastered all the usual problems of life is the single characteristic that disturbs some of his friends who would like to feel closer to him, but find that their efforts to do so don't succeed. His life is steady and level except for recurrent headaches, which, on the advice of his physician, caused him to consult with me.
>
> **Marie:** "Short and shy" lived in the same apartment house I lived in when I first moved to California. She was no more than twenty years old when I first met her. For two years, sensing her shyness, I did no more than nod to her when we passed each other in the hall. After we accidentally ran into each other coming out of a movie house that was showing Roman Polanski's film, *Repulsion*, the story of a young woman who is seductive toward men, but kills any man who tries to have sex with her, we exchanged a few words when we saw each other in the hall. That progressed to her becoming a client of mine after I left the apartment house where we met.

To help you formulate your responses to whichever of the seven central and fifty two helping questions you select, I have recorded at least one person's response to each question. I recommend that you write out your responses to which ever of the helping questions you elect to respond to and give a title summarizing your response(s) to whichever of the central questions you respond to. Your responses to all of the questions you choose to respond to constitutes your **self-narrative**. The titles you assign will help you to respond with maximum productivity to the book's final question, *Who Do You Want To Become?* Here are the titles Anthony gave to his responses to each of the Central Questions:

One	"A Life Built on a Lie"
Two	"A Stimulating-Stunting Childhood"
Three	"An attorney for Justice or the Mafia"
Four	"My Search for Myself"
Five	"Learning to Use Emotion Constructively"
Six	"A History of My Love and Sex Life"
Seven	"From Emotional Pain to Self-Knowledge"
Eight	"From Self-Righteous to Self-Affirming"

Anthony's Self-Narrative appears later in this book under Helping Question 7.2.

Helping Question 1.1:

What Do You Know About Your Family of Origin and How Does It Affect Your Feeling About Yourself and Others?

Angelica

Angelica's mother took child rearing seriously. She followed the advice of the child rearing experts of her day. She put Angelica to sleep at a scheduled time and was careful not to feed or pick her up no matter how much she cried. Angelica screamed most of the night for three successive nights, after which she finally stopped. This set the stage for the relationship between them.

There was never an easy give and take discussion between Angelica and her mother. An image that sticks in Angelica's mind is of her mother perspiring and looking miserable while doing the family ironing. She ironed everything, including the sheets and her husband's underwear. Her mother made sure that Angelica had appropriate clothing and looked her best at all times. She went without things for herself to bring this about, but was preoccupied with doing what she thought was right rather than relating to Angelica on a person-to-person basis.

Looking good and acting appropriately is a legacy that guided Angelica into adulthood. Unfortunately, she didn't realize, until after a painful divorce, how these guidelines limited her interpersonal relationships. Her emphasis was almost exclusively on how she and her husband looked, rather than who they were. Sensitivity to her own and other's emotions and needs was not part of her mother's upbringing, and it wasn't part of hers. If she told her mother she felt hurt about something, her mother was likely to tell her "Oh, you shouldn't feel hurt by that little thing!" This comment was intended to calm Angelica. Superficially, it did. On a deeper level, however, it inhibited her from recognizing and claiming her own feelings. Certainly her mother had good intentions, but her dismissal of Angelica's childhood feelings markedly interfered with Angelica's emotional growth.

Angelica and her mother have done a lot of living and thinking, most recently by sharing their responses to QUESTIONS. This has helped them become more understanding of each other, which has helped them find a better life individually and in their relationship.

Anthony

Anthony was raised on the lower east side of Manhattan. His parents were immigrants. They lived above the grocery store where they worked. His grandfather owned the building, as well as several others. When Anthony graduated from high school he accepted his grandfather's offer to finance his passage through college and law school.

After graduation from law school, Anthony became his grandfather's legal advisor. He discovered that his grandfather's real estate holdings were only a small part of his grandfather's business. In fact, they were a cover for his real business, which was drug dealing. Anthony was shocked to the core.

When Anthony confronted his parents with his newfound knowledge they also acted shocked, but he later learned through other sources that they had always known. After much soul searching he moved to California, limiting his contacts with them to an occasional telephone conversation (initiated by them), and an annual perfunctory exchange of Christmas cards.

In leaving his family Anthony was acting on George Burns' advice: "Happiness is having a large, loving, caring, close-knit family in another city." His life was improved, except for the development of recurrent headaches.

On the advice of his physician, he consulted with me. I suggested he sign up for an adult education course I conducted at the First Unitarian-Universalist

Church of San Diego. An early manuscript copy of QUESTIONS was the text for the course.

When the class addressed the helping question, *What do you know about your family of origin and how does it affect your feelings about yourself?*, Anthony remained silent. After class I took him aside and commented that he seemed unusually quiet that evening. I asked him if this was due to the question we had been discussing. He nodded his head. "Would you care to tell me about it?" I asked. He was silent for a full minute, then mumbled, "My family are liars, cheats, and hypocrites." I urged him to tell me more. He slowly shook his head.

At the next class meeting Anthony shared his family history with the class. During the following class, he was able to acknowledge the possibility that his family's lying was an effort to protect him and themselves from the truth. "Even my grandfather, though he tried to suck me into his way of life, thought he was helping me. Though he didn't intend it, by having me work for him, he did help me—to know and face the truth about him and my parents." By way of summarizing his overall reaction to Central Question One, *Where Did You Come From?*, Anthony entitled his responses to it: "A Life Built on a Lie."

During a trip to the East Coast two years after our final class, Anthony visited his family for the first time in twenty years. His grandfather was dead. His father, though he suffered from Alzheimer's, still recognized him and greeted him warmly, as did his mother. He didn't have the heart to express his anger and sense of betrayal to his father. He did express it to his mother, who confessed that she had lied to him. His sister had known it for a long time, but never said anything to him or anyone else, obeying the family's unspoken rule against discussing such things.

Anthony arranged a second meeting with his father, mother, and sister. This turned into a tearful, deeply meaningful family reunion.

Marie

Since our roots have such a seminal impact on our personalities, they are certain to affect all our relationships to some degree, especially our most important ones. Sometimes this effect is general, as when it affects our total outlook, and sometimes more specialized, as when it primarily affects specific kinds of relationships, such as sexual relationships. The experience of my one-time neighbor, Marie, is of the latter variety. Marie was disturbed by the movie, *Repulsion*, which we discussed after we saw it together. At that time she asked me if I had ever treated a woman like the one in the movie. I replied that I had treated women with sexual problems, but never one as lethal as the one in the movie. She continued to question me. When I mentioned that I was working on a book, she volunteered to read it. I gratefully gave her a manuscript copy. Sometime later she returned the manuscript to me along with her responses to it. When I read her responses I suggested that she work with me professionally. She readily agreed. We saw each other weekly for the next two years. I will have something to say about Marie throughout this book. Here is the first installment:

Marie's father died when she was five. Following her father's death, her mother had a string of lovers, one of whom she married when Marie was age eight. Marie and her mother moved in with with him. This was a big step forward, socio-economically speaking, and this pleased Marie, but she was even more pleased by the prospect of having a normal family life.

Her new stepfather welcomed her. His friendliness included hugs and kisses, which she especially liked. He became more and more affectionate. When he put his tongue in her mouth and started feeling her body, she didn't like it, but didn't stop him. After a while they were having oral sex. She was scared. In a reassuring tone of voice, he told her that she would get used to it and enjoy it.

Gradually that happened, but she felt frightened and guilty. They had oral sex at least once a week for about three months. Then he stopped. Marie never knew why. She pretended that it never happened, but it strongly affected her attitude toward sex. As a young adult Marie was attracted to men, but if they showed any sexual interest in her she immediately withdrew.

Writing down her half-forgotten secret made it more real to Marie. Reading about other people's family secrets and how the emotional problems they brought on were resolved, gave her hope that hers too could be resolved. How this happened will be explained in CENTRAL QUESTION TWO, YOUR CHILDHOOD, WHAT WAS GOOD, WHAT WAS BAD?

Like Angelica, Anthony, and Marie, you learned the values and traditions of your family from your parents, or other care givers. They learned them from their parents or other care givers. To increase your understanding of family traditions, and their influence, learn as much as you can about the personalities and attitudes of your parents and grandparents. Compare them to your own personality and attitudes. Define intergenerational similarities and dissimilarities.

Mothers and Fathers

Mothers (or those who play the role of mother) are especially important in the earliest years of our lives. The vast majority of us develop our first human relationship with our mothers. This relationship, in one way or another, will influence all of our future human relationships.

Fathers (or those who play the role of father) are as important as mothers, though in Western societies they often choose a secondary role. Robert Bly, in his book *Iron John* has commented on how common "the search for the father" is in Western societies. In feudal societies, sons generally worked alongside their fathers. Consequently, they usually felt closely connected. By shifting fathers from working in or close to home to working in factories or offices, industrial society separated fathers from their children and interfered with their knowing each other. The first task, if there is to be a reconciliation between fathers and sons and fathers and daughters, is for them to get to know each other. What Robert Bly doesn't mention is that today 80% of mothers also work, so that many of today's children are confronted not only with the problem of an almost absent father, but also with the problem of an almost absent mother.

Every parent-child relationship is unique. The examples I give are intended to illustrate their infinite variety while demonstrating basic principles to help you better understand your own unique family relationships.

Exercise 1.1:

Sit down with a family photo album. Look carefully at pictures of members of your family of origin. Review in your mind your relationship with each one. Old thoughts and feelings will be remembered. In the light of your present view of yourself and others, which is almost certainly more mature, reevaluate the thoughts and feelings evoked. This will be something like what Ingmar Bergman did in remembering a past love affair, as portrayed in the film *Faithless*. Hopefully it will have the same effect on you that it had on Bergman: developing greater understanding and insight. This can improve the relationship you recall, and prepare you to approach new relationships without duplicating behavior you regret from that earlier one.If you are a mother or a father, compare the way you are bringing up your child or children with the way you were brought up. Divide an 8 1/2" x 11" sheet of paper in half. On the left half write how you discipline your child or children and on the right how you were disciplined as a child.

To what extent are you repeating old patterns? List any emotional problems you think your child or children has/have and try to assess to what extent (if any) you contributed to those problems. What can you do at the present time to help heal any wounds that you have contributed to? Be realistic, don't put all the blame on yourself. Everyone who is sane is responsible for their own behavior, whatever the contributing factors may be. You will be doing your child a disservice if you assume total responsibility for his/her behavior. Children deserve empathy, as do you, but not a shifting of responsibility from child to parent. Are you emphasizing the healthy aspects and minimizing the unhealthy aspects of what was passed on to you? Be especially careful about understanding how your relationship with a child of your own gender is being affected by your relationship with your parent or parent substitute of your gender. If you are not yet a parent, but are planning to be one, you have a golden opportunity to study your relationship with your father and mother, or substitutes thereof, and decide which portions of those relationships you want to pass on to your children and which you want to be sure you do not pass on.

Extra Mile 1.1:

After responding to Helping Question 1.1, *What Do You Know About Your Family of Origin, and How Does it Affect Your Feelings About Yourself and Others?*, ask the members of your family the same question, in a carefully non-accusatory way. For example, you might say to your grandfather, "I sometimes felt you were angry with members of our family, including me. Were you?" Or explain to your mother, "Although I always knew that you cared about me, there was one time that I felt very hurt by you." (Mention a specific instance). Continue with "How did you feel on that occasion?" If family members are no longer living, ask anyone who knew them how they would describe the relative you are trying to understand. Discuss with your family members any differences between their responses and yours. This will help you either confirm, or modify, or fully accept, your opinions. In any case it will deepen your understanding and move you in a more compassionate and forgiving direction, thereby encouraging healing.

Helping Question 1.2:
How Did You/Do You React To Your Culture and Subculture(s)?

The parents of my longtime friend Aaron come from an old German/Jewish family. They felt the need to preserve their Jewish heritage. They almost disowned him when he told them he planned to marry a Christian woman.

Mary, another friend, had a family completely committed to the American ideal of making money. They did disown her when she joined a Buddhist group.

Though these two people were upset by the censure of their parents, they didn't allow parental disapproval to destroy their lives. They respected their parents, but also respected themselves enough to live according to their own convictions.

After they married, Aaron suggested that he and his new wife meet with his parents and a family therapist. After three such meetings his parents reconsidered their position. Not only did they not disown him, they welcomed his wife into the family.

Mary also suggested family therapy, but her parents refused to consider it. She has been a Buddhist for three years now, and the situation between her and her parents remains the same. Don't be dismayed by this. From my experiences with similar situations, I believe that the chances are good that eventually there will be a softening of positions leading to an eventual reconciliation. Such delayed reconciliation's typically take place at a time of crisis in the parents' or couples' lives. There is often conflict between cultures and subcultures, and even between subcultures within a culture. These clashes were dramatically portrayed in the 1967 book (and 1982 film) *The Chosen*, about the friendship between a boy who was brought up in a Hasidic Jewish family and a boy brought up in an Orthodox Jewish family. For more than a year their friendship languished because the father of the Hasidic boy prohibited him to speak to his Orthodox friend. The Hasidic father lifted this ban when the two families united as American Jews fighting for the independence of Israel.

Intergenerational conflict, if it leads to forcible imposition of one generation's will on another, as happened in The Chosen, is destructive. On the other hand, if it leads to an exchange of views and feelings, the result can be mutual emotional and spiritual growth for both children and parents.

Exercise 1.2:

Pick up a newspaper or magazine. Flip through it looking at pictures and faces and reading headlines. Pick a phrase—"bought into," "rebelled against," or "compromised with" that best describes your relationship with the culture characterized in those pictures, faces, and headlines. Reflect how your posture toward the culture you were brought up in has affected your personality development and whether you're pleased or displeased with the results.

Extra Mile 1.2:

If there is someone in your life with whom you are in conflict, it is quite possibly related to differences in the cultures you were each brought up in. To explore such possibility:

- Get to know the person or persons thoroughly. Focus on differences in your respective familial and cultural backgrounds.

- Try to empathize with the other person or persons. Ask them the questions raised in this chapter. Their responses may change some of your responses to them.

This exploration will often resolve the conflict, but if not, by taking these steps you are certain to learn some things about yourself and them that will soften the conflict with them.

Helping Question 1.3:

What Is the First Role You Remember Playing In Your Family?

Arthur

My client Arthur was precocious. The first role he remembers playing was that of "bright boy." At age six, he received an erector set from Santa Claus. That evening he constructed a toy steam shovel, which he pushed into the living room where his parents and their guests were visiting. Their oohs! and aahs! (accompanied by comments on how smart he was) started him on a path he pursued for most of his life. From "bright boy" he graduated to "bright young man," which led to "intellectual" adult.

"Bright boy" and "bright young man" were gratifying. "Intellectual" was sometimes a source of gratification, and sometimes a source of frustration and disappointment. After his first serious romance broke up, in part because the woman he was in love with at the time complained that he was "too intellectual," he experimented with abandoning that role. He wasn't sure what kind of a person he really wanted to be. Focusing on that, he realized that he didn't want to abandon thinking, but wanted to add love and caring to it. It took a lot of work before he was able to describe his present primary role as "A Thinking Lover."

The first role you can remember playing was bound to be a significant influence on the course of your life. The possibilities are infinite. A few less-than-desirable examples are: pretending to be like a sibling in hopes of getting the attention she/he got; acting like a baby to get attention; making like being a little terror to get attention.

Exercise 1.3:

Often the first role you played persists into adult life. How well do you recall yours? Try thinking of a television family you grew up watching. Perhaps "The Brady Bunch" or "Father Knows Best" or "The Waltons" or "The Cosby Show." Was there a child in any of those families who played your role? The troublemaker, the caretaker, the precocious one, the quiet one? Specify to what degree (if any) you are still playing that role. Decide whether you are O.K. with it. If not, formulate and practice change, until you find a version that you are satisfied with.

Helping Question 1.4:

What Were Your Family's Secrets and Lies?

Tom, a former client of mine, never asked either of his parents why they divorced. Influenced by the above helping question, he finally asked his mother. With obvious reluctance and embarrassment she told him that when his father was drunk he sometimes physically abused both her and him. He knew that his father had an alcohol problem as a young man, but didn't know that he had physically abused both him and his mother. Though shocked, he appreciated his mother's belated revelation. It helped him better understand his father, his mother, and himself. For the first time he had an inkling of why he feared and avoided his father. This enabled him to confront his father with what his mother had told him. His father confirmed its truth, and expressed regret for his immaturity at that time. This enabled Tom to forgive him. Though they didn't become pals, at the time of his death they were both working toward establishing a better relationship. Working on that relationship inspired Tom to start working on his relationship with his own son.

Secrets, Lies, and Attitudes

Some time ago, a young woman consulted me about a personal problem. She couldn't decide whether to stay with her boyfriend, or leave him. Because she told me that she had always had a difficult relationship with her mother, I suggested that she invite her mother to participate in one of our meetings. After observing their interaction, I suggested a private meeting with her mother. In the course of our private meeting, her mother revealed that she hadn't wanted a baby when her daughter was born, though she had come to love her by the time she became a teenager. With further encouragement from me she agreed to acknowledge this in a subsequent joint session. After digesting this information (which took several weeks), and further discussions among the three of us; her daughter realized that her indecision about her boyfriend had deep roots. Though her boyfriend said that he loved her, she felt he didn't "really" love her. The words "I love you" had rung untrue to her all her life. With her mother's revelation she realized that there was good reason why she didn't believe it in her childhood, but that reason no longer applied.

After mulling these facts over for several weeks, she came to realize that, unlike her mother's "I love you" when she was a child, her boyfriend's "I love you" was fully felt. Some months later she married the man she loved, knowing he also loved her.

When parents expose secrets and lies, they often find that what they regard as unforgivable (for example, a secret abortion) is seen by their children as much less serious. Even if children share their parents' opinions of the seriousness of a secret or lie, there is a good chance that if it is acknowledged and discussed the children will forgive them. This almost always helps parents forgive themselves, as happened when Anthony confronted, then forgave, his parents. Parents should, of course, use judgment about when and if they should share personal secrets and lies. Children's ability to understand and forgive varies with their maturity. Some secrets and lies would merely be a burden to children too young to deal with them constructively. Parents should postpone sharing secrets and lies that in their judgment their children are not yet ready to deal with.

Alcoholism and other addictions often are family secrets. It is rarely that family members do not already know these "secrets," but frequently they are not acknowledged. Sometimes lack of acknowledgment is so deep that family members are not aware that they are not acknowledging what, on a higher level of consciousness, they know to be true. In such cases, the effects tend to be especially destructive. This psychological defense mechanism—denial—will be discussed in more detail in CENTRAL QUESTION FOUR, *HOW DO YOU HANDLE DISTURBING FACTS AND EMOTIONS?*

Exercise 1.4:

Pretend you are on your death bed and are being visited by one or more important people in your life. Confess to them a secret or lie that you would like them to know before you die. After that decide if it would be helpful to you to acknowledge and work on it before you die.

Extra Mile 1.4:

After you have done the above exercise, ask someone who is important to you to play death bed with you. Share your confession (above), then ask that person to pretend he/she is on their death bed and ask them if there is something she/he would like to tell you before they die. (This exercise may be especially difficult for you or some of the people you may think of doing it with. If this is the case, try preparing a script of what you will say; ask the other person to prepare a script of what he/she will say, and then exchange scripts.)

Angelica, Anthony, Marie and I responded to Central Question One, its four helping questions, and all the suggested exercises and extra miles. We then discussed it with our spouses. We also discussed with them our opinions regarding the influence of family, culture, subculture, economic, racial, and social status; and whether we wanted to revise any of the opinions we had formed as a result of these influences. These activities not only helped us improve our relationships with those of our parents who were still alive, but also deepened our relationships with our spouses.

To summarize CENTRAL QUESTION ONE, *WHERE DID YOU COME FROM?*, let's think of constructing a building as a metaphor for constructing a mature emotional life. The material covered in responding to this question is analogous to the plot of land upon which the building will rise. We didn't select the land, it was assigned to us. If our emotional foundation doesn't rest on solid ground for constructing emotional maturity, it is like trying to build a structure on sand. We may have to accept such limitations, such as bad experiences and resultant insecurities (often called emotional blocks), hopefully without blaming ourselves. It would be unreasonable to expect that limitations in the land we have been given to build on will not cause limitations in the building we have constructed.

I often tell my clients, and anyone else who will listen (I hope you are one) that who you are at present doesn't matter nearly as much as who you are becoming. Think of yourself as an architect who, forced to build on a sandy spot finds a way to do it. Bad experiences and insecurities are like being forced to build upon sandy soil. You can learn to mix that sand with lime and water making it into cement, providing a firm foundation for additional structures that may be necessary to build a better life.

The next chapter, CENTRAL QUESTION TWO: *YOUR CHILDHOOD AND ADOLESCENCE; WHAT WAS GOOD, WHAT WAS BAD?* will help you to further examine your foundation, and learn ways to firm it up. By age six all of us have developed a distinctive style of interaction with our world. This earliest style has a huge effect on the kind of human being we become. CENTRAL QUESTION TWO focuses on understanding and deciding whether the style of interaction you learned in your family of origin is O.K. with you. If not, insight and individual effort can change it, as Marie's, Anthony's, Angelica's and other's responses will demonstrate.

Your responses to some questions will recall painful feelings. But remember that the things that make you cry can also make you laugh. So keep your sense of humor. Consciously try to think of the humorous aspect of the things that make you cry. Though I agree with Socrates that the unexamined life is not worth living, I also agree with a colleague who is fond of declaring "the over-examined life is no life!" In the midst of your most serious moments of searching for self-understanding, don't forget that a good laugh may bring the greatest insight, not to mention the greatest release.

CENTRAL QUESTION TWO

YOUR CHILDHOOD AND ADOLESCENCE: WHAT WAS GOOD, WHAT WAS BAD?

Children have never been very good at listening to their elders, but they have never failed to imitate them.

—*James Baldwin*

Marie

After reading this chapter of QUESTIONS Marie had a dream. In her dream she was sold into the harem of a sultan. She wanted very much to be accepted by the other wives in the harem. Since they were her only source of emotional support, she met the sultan's sexual demands, as they did, though she experienced them as humiliating. This dream was a turning point for Marie. As she put it:

"I knew right away what the dream meant. As a child, I allowed my stepfather to abuse me sexually because I wanted to be accepted into my new family. A sell-out."

Marie realized that she had been unconsciously replaying this childhood nightmare with her husband in the role of seducer; except she often changed the finale by refusing his sexual advances. This is what she wished she had done with her stepfather. She kept going through this altered scenario with her husband in a fruitless effort to relieve herself of the guilt she felt vis-à-vis her childhood sexual relationship with her stepfather. This hopeless effort to resolve her emotional conflict became a symptom of the conflict itself. She couldn't get rid of it because she hadn't been able to distinguish between what was appropriate to hold herself accountable for as a child and what was appropriate to hold herself accountable for as an adult. Stimulated by her dream, in the context of her response to Central Question Two, she finally made that distinction. She could then use her adult reasoning to understand that it wasn't her fault. At the time it occurred, given her emotional maturity at age eight, she handled it in the only way she could.

She continued to work on QUESTIONS and got her husband to work on them with her. They shared aspects of their lives they had never shared before, notably, their premarital love and sex life. This enabled them to establish a love and sex life that was gratifying for both of them, and greatly improved their overall relationship

I know of no one who remembers the moment of their birth, but it is almost always vividly remembered by other family members. Usually they are glad to share their impressions. From their recollections you can recreate the world you were born into. Unfortunately, family members are often reluctant to admit to ambivalent, frightened, or negative feelings, but these often can be inferred. Some of us, because of death or disruption of our families, will have to find non-family members to help us recreate our early childhood.

I had one student who was almost choked to death by her mother. Another was nearly drowned in the family bath tub by an older brother. Most people are not subjected to such dramatic and damaging interactions, but we all have experiences with others that leave us with mild to severe emotional wounds and resulting inhibitions.

Helping Question 2.1:

What Is Your Most Significant Childhood Memory?

When Mary, as a child, asked her mother how she felt about her as compared to her younger brother, Adam, her mother replied that she loved them both equally. "But," thought Mary, "for Adam there is no bed making, no dishes, no early curfews!" Mary felt this preferential treatment meant he was loved more than she was, but she was afraid to say so. Because Mary didn't dare challenge her mother, she couldn't openly express, or even fully realize, her resentment. It took many years, a failed love relationship, and feelings of isolation and loneliness for her to seek help with this problem through joining a narrative therapy group. Her experiences in the group led her to a thorough self-exploration in which she first recognized that she often expressed anger and resentment without being aware that she was doing so. From there she undertook the arduous task of confronting her mother. This helped both of them to come to a more honest and productive way of dealing with each other, as well as other important people in their lives.

When I ask my clients to tell me their earliest memories they often respond with warm reminiscences of their parents, siblings, peers, and others. Some are too trusting and too dependent as a result of early childhood experiences. Later in their lives they have difficulty recognizing and handling coldness and betrayal. Others, like Marie and me, experienced significant childhood trauma and/or neglect and have trouble recognizing and accepting love and care. Childhood memories can become life themes.

Exercise 2.1:

Recall something you did or were involved in as a child that you later came to feel feel was disgraceful. Imagine you're on trial. You must explain yourself to the jury. What is your defense? What do you think the jury will decide? What can you do to release or rehabilitate yourself?

Extra Mile 2.1:

Recall something that was done to you that you feel was disgraceful. If it resulted in a lowering of your self-esteem, or otherwise interfered with your emotional growth, devise a plan for changing that result. You could, for example, search in a catalog of videos for a video that is related to the wrong that was done to you. Watching that video might stimulate an insightful dream, as reading this chapter did for Marie. If you get stuck, share your problem with your best friend, and ask for her/his help.

Helping Question 2.2:

What Formal and Informal Roles Did You Play In Your Family Of Origin?

Everyone I have asked has been able to identify the distinctive roles they played in their family of origin. They have an infinite range. Some of the more common ones are: peacemaker, mother's or father's ally, family hope, fixer, scapegoat, servant. When the role fits the personality of the person playing it, the results are generally positive. When it doesn't, the results are generally negative. An example of the first situation is one of my clients whose father trained him to be a great athlete practically from birth. Since he was well-coordinated and loved sports, he and his father established and maintained a mutually gratifying relationship. An example of the second situation is another client whose father had the same ambition for his son, who wasn't well-coordinated and didn't like sports. They wound up alienated and estranged.

Our ability to select our own roles is very limited until early adolescence. Before adolescence we are not sufficiently developed intellectually or emotionally to play them in any way significantly different from as directed, or in reaction to the directions of a varying mix of family, society, culture, and genetics. After adolescence the vast majority of us are intellectually and emotionally developed enough to become the directors of our own lives. We don't always do so, however, for a variety of reasons, some of the most important of which are touched on by the responses of Marie, Anthony, Angelica, and me.

Ken

During my adolescence, the role of "Older Brother" became preeminent for me. My sister developed severe emotional problems in her teens, which resulted in a suicide attempt. My mother and father, ashamed and overwhelmed by my sister's problems, assigned the job of dealing with arrangements for her hospitalization and eventual release to me. The role I played at that time is known in professional circles as that of "Family Healer"—the family member who is expected and expects to cure the problems of the family.

The role of "Family Healer" is an example of an informal role. Informal roles are more idiosyncratic than the formal ones of wife or husband, brother or sister, son or daughter, mother or father. Informal roles, unlike formal roles, have no definite limit, and are not defined by genetic or legal factors. In addition to family healer, they include such roles as know-it-all, despot, soft touch, joker, tough guy, clown, intellectual, bumbler, ignorant, stupid, selfish, etc.. They are often unacknowledged. As a result we are often unaware that we are playing them, though they frequently have an effect that transcends those that are assigned by society and culture.

I have had a number of male clients who were keenly aware of their responsibilities as fathers and diligently discharged them. Some of them, however, were not aware that they required themselves to always be right when they played the father role, even though they didn't require that of themselves in other roles. Such men often play imperious, authoritarian roles in their relationships with their children. When I bring this to their attention, usually they are initially defensive, often deny it, and sometimes leave therapy. If we have established a firm and trusting relationship, they hang in, deal with their sense of shock and shame, and become eager to eliminate anything destructive to their children.

Exercise 2.2:

List all the formal and informal roles you have played in the course of your life in chronological order in two separate columns. Consider the progression of formal and informal roles you have listed.

- What do you expect your next formal role to be? Self-supporting adult? Spouse? Parent? Senior Citizen? (to name a few). What measures are you taking to prepare for it?

- Are there any informal roles you want to change? e.g. Grouch?, Complainer?, Dependent Person?, Super-Independent Person?

- Are there any informal roles that you want to add? If so, what is your plan for doing so?

Helping Question 2.3:

Did Your Family Live by the Values They Professed?

Anthony

Anthony's parents never discussed ethical dilemmas. They projected an image of themselves as virtuous and law-abiding, though their actions were clearly short of that image. For example, Anthony's father devised a way of by-passing the electric meter in the basement of their store so that they were only charged for a fraction of the electricity they used. Anthony saw the device and suggested a way to improve it. His father denied its existence. After that, it disappeared.

Anthony was crushed when his father rejected his suggestion for improving the device to cheat the electric company and was puzzled that his father denied its existence. It never occurred to him, at the time, that such a device was illegal and immoral. Children crave parental love. Each of us needs affirmation and encouragement from our caregivers. Anthony was no exception in making that his first priority.

Values

It is important to be aware of your values, and at least equally important to determine whether you are actually living by them. Understanding your values and where they came from will help.

Psychological research and clinical evidence agree that our behavior, with its implicit values, is patterned on the behavior of the first important people in our lives. These are almost always members of our immediate family. Identifying the implicit and explicit values of the elders in your life is the most logical way to begin an effort toward clarity. It wasn't until Anthony worked on Helping Question 2.4 that he systematically applied himself to this important task.

Idiosyncratic family-of-origin factors are often reinforced by the culture in which we live. If anyone had asked Anthony's parents whether they thought men and women were equal, Anthony is sure they would have said "of course." If anyone had asked him, as a child, he might have been more innocently forthright and replied that he thought boys were better than girls. By the time he was an adolescent he vigorously proclaimed that men and women are equal, though he acted as though men were superior, as did his mother and father. What he saw in the movies, read in history books, and heard on the radio and in church reinforced this unconscious value. Even though he consciously repudiated it, he lived by it in his relationships with his wife and daughter. Becoming aware of this was the beginning of the difficult and sometimes painful process of changing this less than admirable value on a behavioral as well as an intellectual level.

Exercise 2.3:

Watch a movie that deals with parental self-images and how they can interfere with their and other people's lives (e.g., the movies *Mr. & Mrs. Bridge*, *A River Runs Through It*, *Home For the Holidays*). Then write a story (based on your observations of your parents and yourself) about how your parents' and your self-images affected your relationship. Then imagine how your and/or your parents' self-images could be changed so they would improve your relationship.

Extra Mile 2.3:

If, in your perception, there was a striking difference between how your parents described themselves and how you would describe them, confront them as gently and sympathetically as you can, with this discrepancy. Hopefully, they can acknowledge and profit from such confrontation. This will make it easier for you to approach the job of confronting discrepancies between your own behavior and values, which may have been stimulated by your parents or by other factors in your life. Wherever such discrepancies began, becoming aware of them is the first step toward a higher level of emotional honesty and personal integrity.

Helping Question 2.4:

Were Your Siblings Your Friends?

When Kevin moved into his mother and stepfather's home at age nine, he didn't immediately meet Walter, his stepfather's son from a previous marriage. Kevin described their eventual meeting and subsequent relationship as follows:

"Walter spent his summers at the seashore with his uncle. My mother, new stepfather, sister and I visited him there. As he walked toward us, a handsome, muscular young man in a bathing suit, a friend of my stepfather commented 'What a specimen!' That was my introduction to Walter. I agreed with the assessment of my stepfather's friend. I didn't realize that my admiration was not reciprocated, and didn't register the cool reception Walter gave me.

"When school started a week later, Walter came to live with us. This precipitated nightly arguments between my mother and stepfather. Mother quoted Walter as saying that he didn't want a brother and sister, it reduced his inheritance. She complained that he treated her like a cleaning lady, which he did. At one point the fighting grew so intense, my mother left the house taking me and my sister with her to a hotel. The next morning she confided that she thought her absence would force our stepfather to order Walter to treat her with more respect.

"Apparently it worked, because we returned the next day and heard no more nightly battles. But my difficulties with Walter continued. I sadly remember one evening when we did the dishes together. He smiled at me as though we had established a secret alliance. There was friendliness in this encounter, but it was far from a secret alliance. On another occasion he and some of his friends played touch-tackle football with me and some of my friends. This too, I took as a gesture of friendship. I completely missed the patronizing quality which characterized both of these encounters.

"Walter was an important figure in my childhood and early manhood. I wanted to be like him. His suave, superficially friendly manner and my capacity for self-deception led me to think, by the time we were both in our forties, that he had accepted me as a brother. He hadn't, and never would. After reexamining this part of my life, I was finally able to accept this fact and live in peace with it."

Siblings

When siblings are close in age, especially if they are of the same gender, competition is often a prominent aspect of their relationship. Sometimes it is open and obvious, but more commonly it is thinly veiled.

A college professor talked with me on and off for a year and responded to all the questions in this book before he was able to give up his need to best his brother, a successful professional comedian. He has now given up trying to be a standup comic while teaching, an ambiguity that had threatened his professional future.

It took another client, a twenty-year-old woman, over a year in group therapy to stop trying to beat her older sister in tennis. Only after giving up that compulsion was she able to devote herself full time to classical ballet, which interested her for itself.

Relationships with siblings, like all relationships, vary greatly from family to family. I've worked with some people whose siblings were a central source of strength and support. I've also worked with some who have been sexually and physically abused by siblings, and some for whom competition with a sibling was the main theme of their lives.

Exercise 2.4:

Imagine that each of your siblings are getting married. Imagine further that the intended of each sibling asks you for advice regarding their spouses-to-be. Project yourself into a scene where you talk to each intended about the sibling they are about to marry by explaining the effect that sibling has had on you. If you don't have any siblings, legal or otherwise, consider how it felt to be an only child and go through the above by imaginings regarding others who played sibling-like roles in \your life.

Explain the change you would like to see in that sibling and make an assessment of whether that change is likely or even possible, and if so the best plan for bringing it about. What changes would you have to make to increase your chances of improving your relationship with each sibling?

Extra Mile 2.4

Were you, like Mary, discriminated against because of your gender, or because you, like Kevin and Walter, were only legally siblings? Do you have problems with siblings or those who play, or played, a sibling-like role in your life? Would you like to change this situation? Decide what you think would be the best way to bring about the change you desire. If it doesn't work, make another plan. If plan B doesn't work, don't give up. Wait until something occurs that might help bring about the change you would like, and try again at that time. Remember that a successful change in any relationship requires both parties to change, though not necessarily to the same degree. You can modify your behavior, but you can only stimulate others to do the same. They can't or won't. In that case, accept them as they are and continue the relationship on their terms, if it is tolerable and has some value for you.

Helping Question 2.5:

Were Your Peers Your Friends?

Angelica

It was no accident that Angelica's friends were all female. She never learned to be comfortable with men. She bought into what she was taught, that women should focus on being attractive to men, and shouldn't argue with them. She was, therefore, like her mother, ill equipped to address the inevitable tensions that arise in male-female relationships.

In her thirties, after divorcing her first husband, Angelica worked as a legal secretary. The staff of the law office where she worked became her peer group, and through her association with them she learned a different way of viewing the world. Until then she uncritically accepted the values of her family and mainstream American society. The law office staff was socially and politically radical. Politics was defined in the broadest sense—the way you live your life is a political statement. In that atmosphere she began to question her personal goals and values. Her subsequent contact with QUESTIONS helped her explore her life more thoroughly. Gradually Angelica grew into living by the goals she herself formulated, and only those of her parents which she had examined and found acceptable.

Angelica now has two close male friends. She feels free to respond to them openly. She has given up the crippling idea that women shouldn't argue with men.

Fortunately we have more than one chance to gain emotional support. If we don't get it from our parents, we may get it from siblings. If siblings or parents don't provide it, we may get it from peers. Each type of relationship is influenced by its predecessor(s). Keeping this in awareness can help new relationships become improvements upon rather than repetitions of earlier ones.

Anthony

Anthony was unprepared for life in school. His classmates, sensing his vulnerability, made fun of his ragged clothes and general ineptness. He felt miserable, but managed to get through the first term of the first grade.

During the second term of the first grade Anthony was in a school yard fight. He landed a solid punch on his opponent's nose. To his shock and surprise, blood spurted from his adversary's nose. Anthony stopped fighting. Out of respect for his fighting ability, his classmates stopped making fun of him, but did not befriend him.

At age eight, Anthony made his first friend, a neighbor by the name of Irving. Irving and Irving's parents treated him as part of their family.

Anthony's own parents neglect of him showed in his ragged clothes. One day, in a rare moment of thoughtfulness, Anthony's father bought him a new shirt. He proudly wore it to school, pleased with his newfound respectability, and even more pleased that Irving was as happy for him as he was for himself. Since then, Anthony has always had a best friend. This spared him the severe social isolation he would have otherwise experienced. When he got to junior high he made friends with one of his teachers, which also helped.

Any fighting Anthony does now is verbal only. He has developed a powerful voice, an extensive vocabulary, and has a law degree. These advantages can be deadly when used against those without them, and can lead to metaphorical bloody noses. He's no more comfortable with such symbolic bloodletting than he was with the physical bloodletting of his childhood. With the help of his later life experiences, he has learned how to be respected by others without damaging them. His title for his overall reaction to CENTRAL QUESTION TWO, *YOUR CHILDHOOD AND ADOLESCENCE: WHAT WAS GOOD, WHAT WAS BAD?*, was "From Misery to Tolerance."

Exercise 2.5:

Fold an 8 1/2" x 11" sheet of paper into thirds, producing three columns. In the first column list all the people you currently regard as your peers. In the middle column summarize the nature of your relationship with each one of them. In the third column note anything you wish was different in each of those relationships. Visualize going through whatever you believe you and they would have to do to bring about such changes. Record these visualizations on a separate sheet of paper and make an effort to bring them about. Be prepared to change your mind about ways of bringing about change as you proceed with this effort.

Extra Mile 2.5:

You may be overly dependent on your peers or too aloof from them. Choose a peer you feel alienated from and work on improving that relationship. As with Anthony, this may be the lever for improving your relationships with all your peers. Perhaps one or more of your current peer relationships should be terminated.

Along with work on your peer relationships I recommend work on your current relationships with your parents if they're still alive. See if you are able to say "yes" or "no" to them when warranted, free of any compulsion in either direction. Accept their limitations without being controlled by them. If your parents have died, choose someone whose personality resembles that of one of your parents and work toward establishing a good relationship with that person. Anthony's mother-in-law, for example, with whom he and his wife often had dinner early in their marriage, had a habit of calling everyone to dinner while continuing to do various things in the kitchen. The rest of the family felt compelled to wait for her before they started eating, sometimes for ten to fifteen minutes. Anthony, realizing that this was controlling behavior on the part of his mother-in-law, similar to what he had experienced vis-à-vis his father. After suffering through it a couple of times, he started eating shortly after sitting down. The rest of the family soon followed his lead. No one said anything to his mother-in-law, but she soon discontinued her delay in seating herself.

Bad experiences you have had in the past, and will have in the future, are among the many "negative" experiences that can be regarded as treasures locked in a chest. Find the key, unlock the chest, and draw upon its contents to help you learn how you can become who you want to be. In other words, use such treasures to increase your emotional maturity.

Having explored some of the early influences on emotional development, you are now ready to explore Part Two, Challenges to Attaining Emotional Maturity, which starts with CENTRAL QUESTION THREE, *HOW DO YOU HANDLE ANGER, FEAR, SADNESS?*

PART II

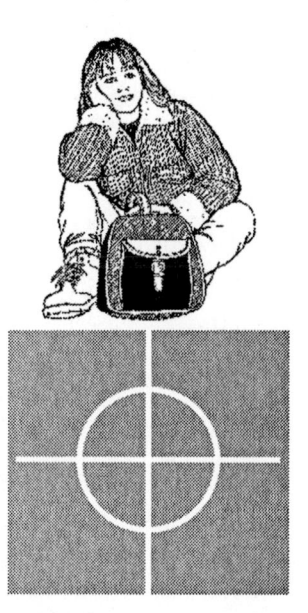

Challenges to Attaining Emotional Maturity

o o o o o o o o o o o o o o o o o o o o o o o o o o o o o

There is a cry deeper than all sound
Whose serrated edges cut the heart as we break open
To the place inside which is unbreakable and whole
While learning to sing.

—*Rashni*

As I hope you have already discerned, the central theme of this book is increasing emotional maturity through becoming more aware of, and altering your self-narrative where you think it should be altered.

Under favorable circumstances (which are usual in the case of physical growth) physical maturity comes into being without special effort.

Under favorable circumstances (which are more unusual in the case of emotional growth) emotional maturity also comes into being without special effort.

Because favorable circumstances are more unusual in the case of emotional growth than in the case of physical growth, QUESTIONS deals mostly with factors which can interfere and hold it up: how to define such factors and make the special effort which is required to overcome them. Its central objectives are turning your:

- fears into sensible precautions
- pain into compassion
- anger into understanding
- sex drive into love
- errors into learning

The two chapters of Part One, Your Early History, dealt with the first challenge: recalling significant incidents that occurred while you were growing up and learning how they affected you. The three chapters of Part Two, Challenges to Attaining Emotional Maturity, deals with the second challenge: attaining control of factors that interfered, and possibly continue to interfere, with your growth toward emotional maturity.

Part One focused on childhood and adolescence; Part Two focuses on adulthood.

CENTRAL QUESTION THREE

HOW DO YOU HANDLE ANGER, FEAR, SADNESS?

Half our mistakes in life arise from feeling where we ought to think, and thinking where we ought to feel.

—*John Churton Collins*

Anthony

Anthony wet his bed from age nine to eleven. No one, least of all he, interpreted it as caused by fear. In situations where it would be appropriate to feel fearful or sad, Anthony felt anger instead. While at summer camp at age eleven, a fellow-camper made fun of him for wetting his bed. Anthony challenged him to a fight, which he won. He acquired a reputation at camp for being a quick-tempered and angry boy. He grew from there into a quick-tempered and angry man. The beginning of his emotional liberation started when, in his QUESTIONS group, his anger was received and welcomed rather than reacted to. In discussing this with his group, he got his first hint that some of his anger might have the purpose of shielding him from other more painful feelings.

A member of his QUESTIONS group asked him to describe his mother. He described her as emotionally subdued, except for occasional flashes of temper that revealed strong currents beneath the surface. For example, when he was eleven, he stepped on the wet kitchen floor she had just finished scrubbing. She slapped his face. He was stunned, not by the force of the blow, but by the fact that she slapped him at all. She had never done that before, and never did it again. On another occasion she cut his fingernails, presumably to improve his appearance. She cut so close it hurt him. She didn't stop when he cried out. Again he was shocked; she could be cruel without provocation.

Reflecting on his responses to CENTRAL QUESTION TWO, *YOUR CHILDHOOD AND ADOLESCENCE WHAT WAS GOOD, WHAT WAS BAD?*, he realized that he couldn't recall a time when his mother said she felt hurt. She converted hurt into anger, and he did the same. He was humiliated and hurt when the kids at camp laughed at him for wetting his bed, but felt better bullying them, rather than letting them and himself know what he was really feeling.

During weekly meetings of his QUESTIONS group Anthony struggled with his one-note expression of feeling. Finally, with the support of the group he took his first faltering steps to end the way he had tyrannized himself and those close to him. Gradually when he felt sadness or fear he was able to weep and share, rather than masking those feelings with rage.

To the quotation which introduces this chapter, "Half our mistakes in life are from feeling where we ought to think, and thinking where we ought to feel," I would add that if feeling and thought are both engaged the results are usually even better than if the "right" one prevails.

Human emotions evolved before human thinking, and they often exert more power. Both are vital signs of human life. When there is incongruity between them, with appropriate effort one or both can be modified so they reinforce each other instead of interfering with each other.

Emotion oftentimes dominates, as with Anthony, but sometimes it is thought that dominates, as we saw with Dan in the preceding chapter. Both got in touch with their particular incongruities, traced those incongruities back to factors in their childhood, and were thereby able to make healthy changes in their thoughts, feelings, or both. This resulted in greater congruity between thought and emotion, which, in turn, resulted in substantial improvement in their relationship to themselves and others.

In CENTRAL QUESTION THREE, *HOW DO YOU HANDLE ANGER, FEAR, SADNESS?*, we will consider each of these emotions in turn, followed by considering whether your thoughts and feelings reinforce each other, and if not, how to help them do so.

Helping Question 3.1:

Do You Get Mad Instead of Sad; Forbear Instead of Share?

Angelica

Angelica grew up in a family in which the expression of strong feelings was implicitly forbidden. As she put it:

"I never saw my parents in a heated argument. All emotions seemed muted and under control. They could express pleasure but not joy, irritation but not anger, sadness but not despair."

"Anger was expressed indirectly by coldness. My mother would not speak to my father for a day at a time if she was aggravated at something he did or didn't do. My father would do the same to my mother."

Although both her parents used coldness to express disapproval or anger, Angelica didn't feel abandoned. If one was distant, the other was usually available to comfort her, but with her mother and father as models, she never learned how to adequately express, much less feel, anger. As a young woman she tended to be anxious and irritable, rather than sad or angry. She had less difficulty expressing positive emotions such as affection or love. The darker, negative emotions were expressed only through coldness, as her parents expressed theirs. Even now, after a great deal of work trying to access feelings, she reports:

"I have to remember to look into myself to uncover the root causes of my feelings. The closer I feel to a person or persons the harder it is for me to define and express my feelings. I remember one time, when I was dating Anthony, he called to change our plans. He later said that I sounded distant on the telephone. He interpreted my defensive distancing of him as rejection.

"Fortunately, at that time, we were both working on QUESTIONS. We discussed his reaction and I was able to acknowledge my contribution to it. What started as an interpersonal problem became an opportunity for us to increase our understanding of ourselves and each other."

Anthony and Angelica are now married (to each other). Exchanging stories about their personal histories and ways of dealing with anger and hurt has helped them understand and deal with each other in a better way than either of them were able to do in their first marriages. When Angelica expresses even a little anger, Anthony encourages her to go into it more deeply, because he knows what she first expresses is probably understated. When Anthony expresses anger Angelica tries not to respond to the anger as such, but tries to help him find what he feels hurt about. She knows his anger may not be the real issue. They have come to think of this as tuning in to each other, turning the volume up or down to help each other improve the fidelity with which they convey their feelings. This has also helped them become less impulsive and more thoughtful and compassionate in their other human relationships.

Angelica and Anthony are aware of the complexity of roles and the hazard of holding on to those that were once useful but no longer are. She is freeing herself of a tendency to be over-involved in the role of mother to her son by her previous marriage, and Anthony is trying to involve himself more as her son's stepfather. Both have recently joined a group studying Marshall Rosenberg's Non-Violent Communication (NVC) and are using it to study, practice, and improve their communication with each other and their children.

Exercise 3.1:

Recall an incident in your life in which you lost your temper in a relationship and subsequently lost the relationship. Review how you would handle that incident (and others) today so as to cause the same outcome to become less likely.

Extra Mile 3.1:

Suggest to someone you would like to feel closer to that you make getting to know each other on a deeper level part of your relationship. It will help you better understand yourselves and each other and increase the intimacy between you. Anthony and Angelica were able to do it, so can you.

Helping Question 3.2:

What Are You Most Afraid Of, and Why?

My client John had such a disturbed childhood that he largely withdrew from reality. By age seven he lived in his own world. He found more comfort there than in the world of reality. When he reached young adulthood he decided to give the real world a chance. He married and had two children. The marriage was a disaster but lasted twelve years. He dated no one until six years after his divorce, when he acquired a girlfriend and was repeatedly awakened by convulsions while sleeping.

His life illustrates both functional and dysfunctional effects of fear. He was born in New York City, the youngest of seven children. After his parents separated, his father took him to a farm in the Midwest. There his father introduced him to a woman he described as "your new mother." His father had married her, though he never divorced his first wife. He told his new wife that John was his illegitimate child. When John asked about his "former" mother, his father told him that his "former" mother was dead.

John was frequently left to wait in the car for his father, sometimes for a half day or more. As a child he couldn't determine what was real and what was not real. Retreating into his own world probably saved him from a mental breakdown, but proved to be an embarrassment later in his life. For example, he got so many F's in school that he was held back twice. In the eighth grade, with the help of a sympathetic teacher, he made progress in returning to the world of reality and for the first time got passing grades in all but one subject. The teacher referred him to a psychotherapist with whom he made further progress.

After his divorce, while still in therapy, John told his therapist, "I can't stand to be touched!" This behavior, a result of his traumatic childhood, was a factor in his first wife's departure.

His convulsions occurred when he dreamed of being physically close to his current girlfriend. They joined a couples therapy group which I led, where he made further progress in embracing the childhood origins of his fear that intimacy led to abandonment. This progress, along with the support of his girlfriend, helped him overcome his fear of closeness. They are now married and he no longer has convulsions while sleeping.

Marie

Marie's childhood was not as disturbed as my client John's, but enough to cause serious problems. Her life illustrates how emotional problems almost always have more than one root.

Marie's father died when she was five years old.

When Marie was eight years old her mother remarried. Marie initially responded to her "new father" as filling the void she had felt since her father's death. Thus she became an easy victim of her stepfather's seduction.

One of the saving graces in Marie's life was that her mother, when pressed, was always honest with her. Unlike John, Marie felt she had someone she could trust. This gave her an anchor in reality. Though she distorted reality in certain ways, as we all do, she never felt compelled, as John was, to create a world of her own.

Everyone experiences interpersonal problems caused by loss of temper or from caving in to fear. These are usually problems of self-control, the development of which is vital for the building of good character and a mature personality. They should be distinguished from problems stemming from lack of insight. Without negating the vital importance of self-control, it may in some cases block insight. This is what happened to John and Marie. They used self-control to avoid experiencing their fears. In a supportive environment, they allowed themselves to experience them. That freed them to gain insight into their origins and realize that though it was once valid for them to repress those particular fears, because they couldn't handle them at the time they were generated. They could now handle them, and did, with the help of the group. After that, they no longer had to repress those particular fears; because they no longer existed.

Exercise 3.2:

Learning how people developed and overcame serious emotional problems can be very instructive even if your emotional problems are much less serious. Considering serious emotional problems is something like looking through a microscope:

ordinary problems are enlarged, which makes it easier to distinguish cause and effect. Look at yourself through the microscope of John and Marie's experiences. What do you see in yourself that resembles what they experienced? Does the resolution of their experiences give you clue as to how to resolve yours?

Helping Question 3.3:

Do You Cry At the Movies?

A Simple Test For Compassion

As a teenager, Angelica sometimes read personal advice columns in the newspaper. She remembers one in which a young girl wrote to a personal advice columnist asking, "How can I tell if my boyfriend is a compassionate person?" The columnist suggested she observe whether he cried at the movies. If he did, the columnist said she would then know he was a compassionate person. If he didn't, the columnist advised caution.

I think that was good advice. At the movies, in the dark, we are more likely to let our feelings show. Our reactions under these conditions are often a truer indication of what we feel than our behavior in everyday life, which is often clouded by self-consciousness and rationalization.

Angelica

Angelica followed the example set by her parents: she did not express her feelings verbally, and, in fact, was often unaware or only partially aware of them. After she observed that Anthony cried at the movies, she felt sufficiently secure with him that she occasionally allowed some feelings to break through in the course of their courtship. Anthony's ability to accept such feelings without recrimination, even when they were directed toward him, helped her free herself emotionally, at least with him. She went from experiencing her feelings with Anthony to expressing them in a women's' support group and finally in other areas of her life.

Hurt is a feeling perhaps most often hidden in our society. It comes in many forms, and like anger and fear, is not a feeling people generally welcome. But, like anger and fear, it is a vital sign of human life. We will confine our attention to psychological hurt: the pain of being unloved, slighted, insulted, or of violating our own standards (guilt). Anger, fear and pain are not emotional problems, but inescapable aspects of living. How you handle these feelings can become an emotional problem. It can also be a stimulus for emotional growth, as it was for Angelica and Anthony.

Exercise 3.3:

Fold a sheet of paper in half, long ways. On the left side list the major hurts you have experienced. On the right side, next to each hurt, summarize how you handled that hurt, what effect it had on you at the time, and what effect it has on you presently. Wherever you have listed a negative effect that persists to the present day, reconsider it in the light of the fact that everything that happens to you can teach you something of value. Record what value that event could have when you reconsider it in this way. Act on that and experience its effect—sometimes the most painful experiences teach us the most.

Helping Question 3.4:

Are You Tormented by Guilt?

The Young Psychologist

A former student of mine was trying to get a psychotherapy practice started. Because she needed clients, she accepted all comers, some of whom had emotional problems beyond her competence. She nevertheless took them on, and felt guilty. After some serious self-examination, she finally took only those she knew she could handle, referring those that were beyond her competence at the time they were referred. This caused some financial loss, which was more than offset by what she gained by establishing ethical professional boundaries.

Guilt is a common form of pain. Like anger and fear, it has acquired a bad name. Irrational guilt, like irrational anger or fear, is an emotional problem. But when rational it is a signal that we are violating our own sense of right and wrong, which can provide the motivation to correct and/or make up for such violations. Not only does this course of action alleviate guilt, but it builds stronger character and makes a contribution to spiritual development.

A growing problem in current American society is lack of guilt, producing what psychologists call sociopaths. An example is the character in the Coen Brothers 1996 film *Fargo* who kills a policeman with as little emotion as killing a fly. Though it's very unlikely that anyone reading this book would be so classified, we all have undeveloped parts of ourselves that can be described as sociopathic. I've had male clients who, without the slightest guilt, routinely told women they loved them in order to encourage them to have sex. I've had female clients who, apparently without the slightest guilt, pretended interest in things that didn't interest them at all in order to encourage men to continue to date them.

Your guilt is irrational if you believe feeling jealousy, greed, and/or anger is abnormal. I hope you will reconsider that mistaken belief and thereby free yourself of irrational pain. If your guilt is rational its resolution will require a change in something you are doing to create it.

Marie's guilt over being seduced by her stepfather when she was a child was caused by her blaming herself for that seduction. Reviewing this incident as an adult, she was able to realize that it was her stepfather, not her, who did something wrong. That helped, but she was still unable to drop her sense of guilt, though she knew it was irrational. After her stepfather's confession and apology she was finally able to drop her sense of guilt emotionally as well as intellectually.

My student, the young psychologist, on the other hand, felt rational guilt because she misrepresented her range of competence as a psychotherapist. To rid herself of that she had to change what she was actively doing to create it.

Both Marie and my student remained their own best friend while solving their respective problems. As a matter of fact, this helped them do it.

Exercise 3.4:

Fold a sheet of paper in two. On the left side list the major things you feel guilty about. On the right side make an evaluation as to whether your guilt is rational or irrational. For any that you have evaluated as rational, list what you would have to change about yourself to insure that you will not repeat whatever you did in the past that you feel guilty about now. Also list any amends that you can make at the present time. Trace any guilt you have evaluated as irrational, to the primary and secondary events in your earlier life where it began. Sometimes that's enough, but usually more is required, like inventing a mantra declaring your innocence and repeating it every night until you no longer need it.

Extra Mile 3.4:

Discuss any guilt you feel with a trusted friend, or better, with a trusted group, and with any of the persons who were involved in what you feel guilty about. This will give you added clarity and added motivation for change.

Helping Question 3.5:

Do You Con Yourself and/or Others Regarding What You Feel?

I have had a few clients who, when confronted with a loss they can't handle, treat that loss as a joke. This represents an extreme of conning yourself. Sometimes I am able to help such clients and sometimes not. Mr. Y is an example. He invited me to his wife's funeral, which occurred after he stopped seeing me. He was all laughs and smiles with me and the other guests. This wasn't an act in the usual sense. He genuinely believed this was the best way to deal with her death, and I'm sure that, for a time at least, he convinced himself that he really felt as lighthearted as he portrayed himself. This of course, prevented his friends from fully showing their sympathy and thereby further removed him from his pain. By not allowing himself to experience his pain he saved himself from facing it, but made it unresolvable. His suppressed grief will probably break through at some point, and when it does, it will have gained strength. It will drive him into either insight, more serious emotional problems or (hopefully) into the hands of another therapist (we now live across the country from each other).

The 1965 film *The Pawnbroker*, is an excellent portrayal of the tragically self-defeating nature of disconnection from one's true self. A Jewish professor and his family are arrested and sent to a Nazi concentration camp. He experiences many horrors including the death of his wife and two children. He survives and becomes a pawnbroker in the U.S. He successfully suppresses his concentration camp experiences at the cost of cutting himself off from any emotionally meaningful human contact, which results in further tragedies.

In addition to the hazard to ourselves, separating from our feelings is also a hazard to others. It is often very difficult (and sometimes impossible) to know what someone feels if they themselves don't know and give out misleading signals. What such people really feel will be expressed only in situations where they are temporarily caught off guard. This was the case with my client, Mr. Y, whom I spoke of when I introduced the concept coning oneself and others. He expressed his real feelings easily, as long as they were agreeable to his sense of who he was. If one that was not agreeable to his sense of who he was slipped through, he immediately covered it up. If confronted with it, he immediately denied it.

Our personalities develop primarily through identifying with, and copying what the people and institutions that surround us say and do as we grow up. This includes our family, our culture, our nation, and the world, in that order. These important influences affect us before we have developed self-awareness. Consequently, as adults, they are generally part of our unconscious. The authorities in all of these groups exert the greatest influence, so it's best to start with exploring the effects of whoever in your family, culture, nation, and the world had the greatest authority in your eyes, and the ways in which you identified and fought with them.

Exercise 3.5:

Review the history of your relationship with your parents as developed in responding to the preceding five helping questions. If one of your parents was the principal authority in your family, reflect on why that was so. If they had equal authority, did you respect one more than the other?

- In what ways do your present attitudes resemble those of your parents?
- In what ways does your current behavior resemble theirs?
- Are you content with the ways in which your attitudes and behavior resemble, or don't resemble, theirs? If not, make a plan that you think will lead to greater contentment; and practice it until it does.

Helping Question 3.6:

Who Were/Are Your Models For Handling Early Emotions?

Brian

Like everyone else, my client Brian had conscious and unconscious models as he grew up. His conscious models evolved from The Mechanical Man, to Korak the Killer (son of Tarzan), to Louis Pasteur, to Jonas Salk. His unconscious models were his father and mother. Brian didn't become aware of the influence of his unconscious models until he found himself behaving toward his son, Archie, as his father had behaved toward him. If Brian did something his father disapproved of, he wouldn't speak to him, sometimes for an entire day.

When Archie first got into trouble with the law, and needed the support of Brian like never before, he and Archie spent an entire day driving back and forth from the courthouse, sitting in the court until Archie's case was called, and then testifying. During this time, Brian didn't say a word to Archie, just as Brian's father would have behaved toward Brian in circumstances like these. This was very discouraging to Archie, as it had been to Brian. Fortunately, later in the week, after a talk with his wife, Brian asked Archie to please forgive him, something his father never did. This and other elements of his family's functioning were encouraging, inspirational even. The Great Depression was a major factor in the lives of everyone Brian knew during the early years of his life. Overall, his family confronted their economic struggles with courage, originality, imagination, and enterprise. When the electricity was turned off because Brian's family couldn't pay the bill, his stepfather bought kerosene lamps and sold mimeographed directions for living without electricity to others whose electricity was turned off. Brian and his sister delivered newspapers and magazines, and his stepbrother largely worked his way through college. The Great Depression years were the best years of their family life. It was a good example, and it served Brian well. Growing up he suffered less fear, especially concerning money, than the average person. He conveyed this to Archie, who put it to good use later in his life.

There was a saying when I was a young man: "If you want to know what it would be like to be married to a particular woman, take a good look at her mother, because that's what she'll be like twenty years from now." I suspect the young women of those times were saying something similar about young men and their fathers. In any case, the observation is valid. There is a great deal of research as well as clinical evidence showing that models and ideals are of critical importance in the development of personality, skills, and over-all sense of competency. There is also evidence that if parents gain insight into unconsciously destructive behavior toward their children and can apologize and change their ways before it is too late, the negative effects of their past behavior can be minimized.

Exercise 3.6:

Make a list of the names of the people who were your models for handling early emotions. Next to each name on your list write a brief description of that person's influence on your behavior and what changes, if any, you would like to make in the effects of their influence upon you.

Helping Question 3.7:

Does Humor Play A Significant Role In Your Life?

Brian's mother, and father, possessed a distinctive sense of humor. His mother and father could be lighthearted and fun-loving. Occasionally his family spent weekends with other families, where together, his mother and father made a good team. His father loved to clown and his mother encouraged and applauded his antics.

Brian's father's sly sense of humor was expressed in wisecracks. He gave people names according to their dominant characteristics: "Frivolous Frances," "Randy Rhoda," "Paunchy Chauncy." His sense of humor won him acceptance into peer groups, which helped to heal some of the wounds caused by his father's rejection of him. Brian adopted his father's penchant for humor by playing the role of a wisecracking clown.

Humor is an important means for achieving and maintaining control and balance. Humor gives us perspective on ourselves and others. It can be very penetrating, and at the same time, can include basic acceptance of the person at which it is aimed. This combination can facilitate self-expression while countering the otherwise often baleful effects of anger, fear, and hurt.

"Laughter is God's gift to mankind," proclaimed the preacher ponderously. "And mankind," responded the cynic, "is the proof that God has a sense of humor."

Exercise 3.7:

If you're like most of us, you could use more humor in your life. Try to think of three ways you could introduce more of it into your life. Perhaps by making up funny names for some of your friends and relatives, like Dan's father. Or more clowning, like his stepfather. Or applauding the humor of others, like his mother. There are countless ways: use whatever works for you.

Extra Mile 3.7:

Consider something you're currently upset about. Probe it for the ridiculous, the comical side, until you can laugh at it (even a little).

Helping Question 3.8:

What Makes You Happiest?

Most unhappiness is caused not by what actually happens to us, but how we interpret what happens to us. A measure of sadness is part of life, and cannot be avoided. An aspect of emotional maturity is not to allow sadness to throw you permanently out of balance.

Removing or reducing sources of unhappiness is, of course, a big help and a part of the path to happiness. Defining what makes you happy is at least equally important, and varies from person to person. It is especially difficult in the American culture, where we are constantly bombarded by advertising telling us what will make us comfortable to blissful. Hopefully we eventually learn that advertising is primarily aimed at making a sale, which is pleasing to the advertiser, but not necessarily to us. All of the people whose lives are outlined or touched upon in this book changed their happiness goals to some degree while going through its questions, exercises, and extra miles. Anthony shifted from running away from people who hurt him to understanding, forgiving, and reconciling with them. Angelica changed from numbing herself to accepting fear as a partner in growth. I abandoned striving for status in favor of striving for emotional maturity. Marie learned to look for quality in men rather than allowing herself to be swept off her feet by sexy men devoid of character.

Exercise 3.8:

Make a list of the things you are striving for in life in the order of their priority. Make a second list of the happiest moments in your life. Compare the first list with the second. Are there strivings on your list that have not led to a better life? If so, consider some shifts, as did Angelica, Anthony, Marie, and Brian.

In CENTRAL QUESTION FOUR: *HOW DO YOU HANDLE DISTURBING FACTS AND FEELINGS?* we will go into detail concerning discovering and overcoming such facts and feelings.

CENTRAL QUESTION FOUR

HOW DO YOU HANDLE DISTURBING FACTS AND FEELINGS?

○ ○

You'd be paranoid too if everyone was against you.

—*Samuel Goldwyn*

Dachau

A friend of mine was with the first company of American soldiers to enter Dachau Concentration Camp during World War II. He told me that at the time he felt no emotion. Three days later, after he had helped bury corpses and helped near-corpses into refugee camps, he broke down and cried for most of an entire day.

The concept of protecting yourself from emotional pain has been intuitively understood for a long time. Shakespeare implied that King Richard III's cruelty was a protection against feelings of inadequacy due to his lameness, and that Lady Macbeth's hand-washing was a protection against feeling guilt about her involvement in the murder of Duncan.

Not being aware of significant feelings becomes a personality problem only when we adopt particular patterns of behavior, or ways of thinking about ourselves and others, that prevent us from ever becoming aware of them.

If my friend, for example, had continued to inhibit his feelings, as King Richard III and Lady Macbeth presumably did, he would never have become aware of them, which would have resulted in stunted emotional growth. This is what is likely to happen if we are confronted by unbearable feelings in our earliest years, as was shown by Rene Spitz and his associates in studies of institutionalized children. Some of the children he studied had received scant attention from their caretakers. Those who had experienced this could not respond to positive, loving gestures from the Spitz Research Team, or anyone else. Some died despite receiving adequate nutrition.

Once unconscious habitual ways of protecting ourselves from unbearable feelings become established parts of our personality, they are automatically activated whenever we feel threatened by such feelings. Some common behavioral practices that most people have outgrown, but may fall back on in times of high stress, are denial, addiction, blaming, psychosomatic illness, rigid role playing, aloofness, disdain, and power seeking. The problem with these behaviors is that though they deaden emotional pain, they prevent us from becoming aware of the true source of our pain. This makes it impossible to work out a productive way of dealing with it. This interferes with, and can halt normal emotional growth. What is required is examination and discovery of habitual patterns of behavior which are self-defeating.

All the exercises in this chapter could be considered "extra mile" exercises in that they require more than the usual amount of effort on your part. I encourage you to do only the exercises in this chapter that you have identified as applying to you. Don't be surprised if you turn up something that you need some help with. As was suggested in the introduction it is good to have a safety net in place before going into the more difficult exercises. A friend, a group, or even a therapist. When you intentionally remove an immature way of dealing with something, change becomes possible, but such change is often accompanied by temporary tears, pain, instability, and/or shakiness.

CENTRAL QUESTION FOUR, *HOW DO YOU HANDLE DISTURBING FACTS AND FEELINGS?*, will help you become aware of the repressed feelings behind any immature way of dealing with your life. The goal is to use whatever you truly feel and use it to stimulate problem solving. Once you become aware of the repressed feelings you are trying to avoid and confront them squarely, you will be and confront it squarely, you will be removing a road block to your emotional growth. This will result in a resumption of normal emotional growth. Becoming aware of the feelings that have caused you to develop such ways of avoiding self-awareness is the first step toward eliminating them. When you first become aware of the feelings you're trying to avoid, you will undoubtedly feel bad; how bad varies from person to person. Hopefully it will be no worse than my friend felt after three days of repressing his feelings. Following that, you, like him, will be in a position to use such feelings to encourage, rather than discourage, your emotional growth. The descriptions of common unconscious self-defeating behaviors outlined in QUESTION FOUR are designed to help you in this effort.

Helping Question 4.1:

Are you a Denier?

Angelica

After her first marriage broke up, Angelica told herself and her friends that she was glad it was over; she knew it was a mistake in the first place. A year later she began living with another man. Her new significant other developed prostate cancer and died two years after they started living together. Again she told herself and others, "I'm O.K., I expected his death and was fully prepared for it." Brave words, but unfortunately a denial of her pain and anger at being left by a man for the second time.

In the course of going through QUESTIONS, Angelica went through a period of tearfully recalling her unhappy childhood and her need not to yield to feelings of frustration and despair. She remembered announcing that she was "the mechanical girl." This denial of her true feelings probably prevented a complete breakdown, but continuing to maintain that image of herself after she was a grown woman made it impossible for her to resolve the feelings of frustration and despair from her childhood and in her current adult life.

As a young woman, she had a recurring dream that she was encased in plaster. She interpreted the plaster as symbolizing the way she protected herself from interacting with people—a metaphorical armor which protected her "mechanical woman" self-image. When she started on QUESTIONS she had a dream that the plaster she was encased in developed some cracks. As she continued, the cracks slowly widened, causing large sections of the plaster to fall off. After going through this chapter she had the following dream:

"I was wearing a coat with many pockets. I wrote my feelings on index cards and put them in the pockets. I did this for a long time. The pockets were overflowing. I suddenly felt the full weight of the coat. It was a burden that was holding me down and preventing me from moving about freely. I realized I no longer needed it, in fact, it had become a handicap. I discarded it, and suddenly felt more spontaneous and happy."

Thinking about this dream Angelica realized that she had been denying feelings of attachment to others for a long time. As was brought out in the discussion of her responses to CENTRAL QUESTION ONE, *WHERE DID YOU COME FROM?*, a significant part of her was stuck in the first stage of emotional growth—symbiosis (complete dependence on others). Getting a job as a young woman helped her to move toward the next stage, separation, (autonomous living). But her habit of denying remaining feelings of dependency through her fantasy as "the mechanical girl," continued. Insight into this didn't result in an immediate suspension of a lifetime habit. Change of this kind takes work as well as time. She still doesn't always immediately recognize her feelings. Sometimes it takes a day or more for her to get in touch with them, but she does express them then, thus giving herself a chance to resolve them in less self-defeating ways.

It hasn't been easy, but her alertness to the pervasiveness of denial in her life has brought her to a much more balanced place about expressing herself. She believes, with justification, that she is now functioning at a significantly higher level of emotional maturity.

Exercise 4.1:

Reflect on any situation that causes you to feel uncomfortable. Pick some key words that describe your feelings regarding that situation. For each of those words write down any words that come to your mind.

- Are there any new feelings when you do this? Try to understand why they didn't arise when you first felt uncomfortable.
- If you continue to do this, you will be able to define the repressed feelings. Go from there to analyzing why you repressed them.
- The final step is to express those feelings and the reasons you had repressed them with conviction but without anger.

A recent incident in Angelica's life is an example of the above process. Her women's group was discussing the question of whether it was necessary to have a majority of members present at a meeting before any decision of importance could be made. Angelica took the position that a majority of the group had to be present. One of the group members countered that if she felt that way it was up to her to devise a way they could always be sure that a majority are present. Angelica felt uncomfortable but said nothing. While the meeting went on she wrote down words that came to her, the principal one of which was "unfair." Along with this word, she realized that she was angry. She felt it was unfair of a group member to arbitrarily try to give her the responsibility of insuring attendance. She realized the the reason she didn't express this, or even feel it, at the meeting, is that a friend of hers had said it. She expressed all this to her friend before the next meeting. Her friend apologized, thanked her for bringing it to her attention, and subsequently apologized to the whole group, leaving her and Angelica closer friends than before and Angelica more able to feel and express her feelings.

Helping Question 4.2:

What Are You Addicted To?

Anthony

When he went to college, Anthony found it was de rigueur to go out with girls, something he had never done, and felt very unsure about. He discovered that having a drink helped him relax, so he took to drinking with enthusiasm, progressing from moderate to heavy indulgence. By the time he was out of college, after several close calls, and one accident while driving under the influence, he realized that his drinking had become a problem. With the help of AA he managed to stop, but put on fifty pounds.

The dictionary definition of "addict" is "to devote or surrender (oneself) to something habitually or obsessively." By this definition, almost everyone is addicted to something. Some addictions are relatively harmless, for example, being addicted to learning or exercise. The defining distinction between dedication and addiction is whether your devotion is motivated by love of the thing itself, or is really a way of avoiding something else. If you love exercise for itself, that is dedication. If you love exercise obsessively, as a way of avoiding something else, that is addiction. Anthony learned in AA that his drinking was an addiction, a way of avoiding painful feelings. He received enough support from AA to stop drinking, but not enough to avoid another addiction, this time to food. The combination of working with AA and QUESTIONS enabled him to precisely define what it was that he was avoiding, first with one addiction and then another. The inner feeling of emptiness that he had felt ever since he learned that his family was supported by criminal activity. His immediate response to that knowledge was to abandon his family, which increased his feeling of emptiness. After he was able to forgive and rejoin them he found himself better able to tolerate emotional pain, and to go from there to learning where the pain came from. He realized, on a deep level, that heavy drinking, by numbing his feelings, had blocked off the means to his salvation. From that point on, when he found himself in emotional pain, he sought to understand and use it rather than block it out with alcohol or excessive eating. The motto of an addict is, "I know how to forget unpleasant feelings." Anthony learned a better motto, "When I feel emotional pain, I will learn what it means and use that knowledge to change my behavior appropriately."

Drugs aren't always used to avoid feelings. In fact, they can sometimes help put you in touch with feelings, as attested by the Latin saying *in vino veritas*, or in the clinical use of sodium pentathol to help people tell the truth when they are resisting doing so. More commonly, however, they are used to deaden the impact of unhappy feelings. The use of drugs (especially alcohol) is well known as a way of avoiding unwanted feelings. It deadens emotional pain. The process of remaining dead to emotional pain requires progressively increased dosages.

I don't mean to imply that Anthony's way of solving this particular problem is the only or best way. It was best for him, and might be helpful to others. I've had clients who solved drinking problems with the aid of Psychoanalysis, Reconditioning Therapy, Primal Scream Therapy, Rational Recovery, and AA, to mention only a few of the hundreds of possible treatments. What is likely to work for any particular person, can sometimes only be discovered by enrolling in a treatment program. There, with the help of the staff and other enrollees, it is easier to formulate a rational plan for a happier life. Sometimes it takes a combination of treatments to overcome serious addictions.

Your plan, if it is to have a lasting effect, must include provisions for developing an overall satisfaction with life, otherwise you may slip into another addiction, as Anthony initially did. If you only stop drinking you may wind up jealous of people who do. As Oscar Levant said, "I envy people who drink—at least they know what to blame everything on."

Exercise 4.2:

If you are a drug user and suspect that you might be addicted, try doing without the drug for at least six months. If you can't accomplish that, you need to enroll in a program to treat your addiction.

Extra Mile 4.2

If you can accomplish the above, it doesn't mean that you don't have a problem, but it is a problem that can be solved through individual effort. Look at a list of possible addictions (you may think of them as obsessions). From this list choose which one(s) you use to avoid pain. Share this with someone you trust. Devise, with their help, a plan for tolerating and using pain constructively, as Anthony succeeded in doing. He turned pain into an asset. A neat trick. With effort, you can do it too.

Helping Question 4.3:

Are You a Blamer?

Marie

At one time in her life Marie had a hospital job with a caseload of dying AIDs patients. The head nurse repeatedly criticized her for getting too emotionally involved with the patients. Marie felt the head nurse was under-involved with patients, and told her so. The tension between them became so intense that Marie left the unit, afraid if she didn't, she'd have a nervous breakdown. Marie's boss, like Marie, was a blamer, someone whose automatic response when she felt threatened was, "It's not my fault, it's your fault!"

When I met her, a year after she left this unit of the hospital, she was still consumed with anger over how badly she thought her former boss had treated her. After learning more about denial, she gave some thought to the possibility that, though exaggerated, her former boss's accusations had some validity. Because she received inadequate care when she was growing up, as spelled out in her responses to Helping Question 1.1, What Do You Know About Your Family of Origin, and How Does It Affect Your Feelings About Yourself and Others? she came to realize that her concept of the role of caregiver was an exaggeration of what was best for her patients. Her boss was under-involved with patients for her own reasons, which exaggerated her complaints about Marie, but didn't invalidate them. Over a period of time, Marie was able to forgive herself, after which she was also able to forgive her former boss.

Denial comes in many varieties, depending on degree of awareness. At one end of the scale is repression: meaning little or no awareness of what is denied. At the other end is suppression: meaning what is denied can readily be brought into awareness.

If you are in a state of repression regarding a particular aspect of yourself, you are a candidate for developing blaming as a way of protecting yourself from becoming aware of that aspect of yourself. Since going through QUESTIONS, whenever Marie feels particularly upset about someone's overt or veiled criticism of her, she looks into whether she's denying something she knows, on some level of her being, is true.

Almost everyone uses blaming to some degree. My advice is that whenever you find yourself blaming someone because of a particular characteristic of theirs, look to yourself. You probably share it, or its opposite. For example, you may blame someone because they are rarely on-time for appointments: it may be that you are too rigid about being on times. The important thing to remember is to use your reactions to help you understand and forgive their shortcomings and your own.

It doesn't mean that you should ignore what you and/or the other person does. It only means that you should practice not blaming that person. If, for example, someone complains that you are unreliable, thank them for telling you, and make an effort to determine whether their complaint is valid. If you decide it is, make an effort to correct it. Making notes to yourself regarding commitments you have made is a good way to start.

Exercise 4.3:

If you frequently mutter under your breath about how stupid people are (in a traffic jam, for example), or if, after a review of your interactions with people over the last three months you find that you consistently blame others for whatever bothers you, you are a blamer. After you have determined that you are a blamer don't blame anyone for anything for one month. If you slip back into your old ways once, start over again. After succeeding in not blaming anyone for one continuous month; if you believe someone is responsible for a particular error, call it to their attention without blame. Focus on what you can do to help them and what you can learn about yourself rather than losing the opportunity of doing something for both of you. If you can keep with this for at least six months you will be well on your way to no longer being a blamer.

Helping Question 4.4:

Do You Have Psychosomatic Symptoms?

Angelica

We all have habitual protections against experiencing emotional pain. In addition to her denial of feelings, from which she is currently recovering, Angelica also suffers from psychosomatic symptoms. The unconscious motto of the psychosomatic is: "Physical pain is better than emotional pain."

Most people would not suspect that Angelica is psychosomatic. She is rarely overtly sick, but since she was a teenager she has had a continuing problem with her GI tract. She didn't recognize the problem for what it was until after consulting with numerous specialists.

Now in her mid-fifties, Angelica is now finally able to acknowledge what some of the medical specialists she consulted suggested, but which she rejected: her physical symptoms are related to her emotions. Stress, tension, and anger can trigger hyperacidity which results in pain, sleeplessness, and a general feeling of discomfort. In recent years she noticed that these symptoms come on very slowly (since they are related to an accumulation of tension and stress). With the help of her responses to CENTRAL QUESTION TWO: *YOUR CHILDHOOD, WHAT WAS GOOD, WHAT WAS BAD?* she recalled that as a girl, illness was the only excuse that succeeded in getting her at least a temporary release from her tough daily chores. Today they are a signal for her to examine what is going on in her life at the time they occur. Such an examination usually leads her to make a change, either in what or how much she's doing or in her perception of what and how much she's doing. This has greatly eased her intestinal symptoms.

Anthony

In recent years, Anthony has been blessed by an absence of psychosomatic symptoms. This was not always the case. While in law school, he developed a headache every Thursday, when students conducted mock trials which were then critiqued by students and faculty. The headaches were a result of emotional conflict: a wish to be well-regarded by the faculty and his wish to express his own opinions, some of which he knew the faculty would not agree with. As he discussed these feelings with his first wife, his nervousness increased and his headaches decreased. This evolution of symptoms, from psychosomatic (headaches) to nervousness (anxiety) was the result of becoming aware of this emotional conflict. As a result of grappling with the actual issue, he decided that, though he respected the opinions of the faculty, if there was a conflict between what they believed and what he believed, he would act on what he believed. When he did so, he was pleasantly surprised to find that, overall, they respected him more rather than less. His nervousness decreased. This personal experience with psychosomatic symptoms also helped him empathize with his second wife, Angelica. Gradually they both have learned to tell the difference between what they should hold themselves responsible for, and what is beyond their responsibility. This has markedly reduced the level of tension under which they function with each other.

These experiences of Angelica and Anthony illustrate, once more, how expressing feelings within a supportive context, rather than suppressing them (for example, by the use of drugs) can lead to greater self-understanding. This increases your ability to resolve issues, reduces discomfort and anxiety, and frees you to enjoy the results of emotional growth. Angelica and Anthony did it, so can you.

Exercise 4.4:

If you have what you suspect are psychosomatic symptoms, go through a thorough medical checkup to be sure there is no physical cause. If you have determined, to your satisfaction, that there is no detectable physical cause, go through a careful review of your self-narrative to help you define the likely emotional cause.

After you have identified what you believe is the emotional cause of your symptoms, reread what Angelica and Anthony did and do likewise. If this too doesn't help, it's time to seek the he help of a professional psychotherapist.

Helping Question 4.5:

Are You a Rigid Role Player?

It sometimes makes sense in everyday life to act differently than you feel. If this is done consciously and for honorable purposes, it is not an emotional problem. If done unconsciously it often is an emotional problem. When acting is done in everyday life there is the danger that if it is done repeatedly, the actor will forget he's acting, and become convinced that this is really him. This was illustrated in the film *A Double Life*, in which Ronald Coleman, playing the part of Othello, got so lost in that role, *he actually did try to strangle the woman playing Desdemona.* Fortunately, her struggles caused him to cease his overdoing of playing the role of Othello.

In the film, *The Remains of the Day*, Anthony Hopkins portrays an English butler whose rigid playing of his role (as an unconscious protection against intimacy) was threatened but never breached. He defined himself as being a butler, not that he simply earned his living as a butler. In the film *Shadowlands*, Hopkins portrays a real life author, C.S. Lewis, who overcomes his protection against intimacy (rigidly playing the role of an intellectual) by realizing that to be open to love he must also be open to pain.

The above examples are fictional and somewhat extreme, but a little reflection should convince you of their plausibility. They both illustrate the unconscious motto of the rigid role-player, "If I act a particular way, I'll be that way." We are all conscious or unconscious actors at times. Insight is not the only way to overcome this and other defenses, but it is often effective, especially when combined with other measures, like practicing playing preferred roles. A bonus is that it can lead not only to the relief of symptoms but to emotional growth as well.

Almost everyone has used rigid role playing as well as other defense mechanisms to some extent at times. Angelica, for example, after she took first place in a beauty contest, began playing the rigid role of a beauty queen. Fortunately, with the help of a high school teacher who befriended her, she got a glimmer of how playing that role got the attention of boys but interfered with making meaningful connections with them. What that teacher told her was reinforced by her experiences during her first marriage. She married a "hunk" and he married a "beauty queen". She quickly discovered that a good marital connection could not be sustained if its principal reason for being is to sustain both of them in the rigid roles they have selected.

Rigid role-playing can be a misuse of legitimate pride. It is not uncommon, for example, for mothers and fathers who have taken legitimate pride in playing their parenting roles well, to insist on continuing to play them after their children are fully grown. In many cases, clinging to such roles is a way of avoiding facing and embracing their appropriate roles as senior citizens.

Exercise 4.5:

If you use rigid role-playing to avoid feelings that threaten you in some way it will take courage to acknowledge it and experiment with being less rigid. You will often feel uncomfortable when you experiment in this way but if you continue, you will become a freer and more open person. There will be an improvement in your relationships with people as well as an increase in your self-confidence, satisfaction, and integrity that will more than compensate for your initial discomfort.

Helping Question 4.6:

Are You An "Above-It-Aller?"

We all know people who use aloofness, or acting above-it-all, sometimes consciously, and sometimes unconsciously. In either case there are unconscious elements operating. If they become aware of the unconscious elements they will realize that even if they have a legitimate reason for rejecting a particular person, their way of doing it is guided by personal defenses. Sometimes they will be rejecting someone who might be of great value to them.

People who use aloofness as their principal protection are, unfortunately, unlikely to undergo psychotherapeutic treatment or involve themselves in a self-help program. The notorious Unabomber is a dramatic example. I believe that he tried to deny his failure in establishing close and meaningful human relationships by isolating himself. A further protection was to convince himself that he is a superior person, justified in using violent means to assert what he believes. He cannot allow himself to feel he is a failure (if he faced that feeling it could be the beginning of his salvation), so he confuses self-protective behaviors with having a real life.

Although no one who reads this book is likely to carry the defense of aloofness to the lengths of the Unabomber, we all may use it from time to time, sometimes with some insight after the fact. For example, Marie, after going to a church service usually socialized with people she knew. However, sometimes she felt vulnerable, assumed an air of aloofness and didn't make an effort to socialize, hoping they would make the effort. Sometimes they did and sometimes they didn't. When no one reached out to her, probably discouraged by her air of aloofness, she later regretted losing the opportunity to make contact. Awareness of her regret and its origin helped her abandon this form of defense.

Exercise 4.6:

Acknowledging the use of aloofness can be painful, but it will be less painful in the long run than continuing to use it. If you suspect that you are using it in any of your human relationships, put yourself on the same level as the person or persons you are using it against and study your inward feelings from that position. If you do that consistently, you will find as Marie did, that this leads to more social success and more pleasure in life.

Helping Question 4.7:

Are You a Disdainer?

Clarence

Clarence's parents expected him to be better than others, just as they felt they were better than others. He, like them, is more intelligent than most according to the results of standardized intelligence tests. This often encouraged them and him to feel disdainful toward others., though a high IQ is far from a measure of overall superiority. After going through the exercises in this book he told me:

"Disdainfulness is unacceptable to me, so I rarely feel it consciously. When I get a revealing signal, such as using a deprecating tone of voice when describing or interacting with someone, I make a special effort to become conscious of where it's coming from. This usually enables me to consider the person it is directed toward in a wider context, which usually results in empathy or at least tolerance. I consider disdain the root of systematic prejudice."

Disdain is more severe and destructive than aloofness. What the disdainer conveys to the person being disdained is, at best, "You're not worth my notice," at worst, "You are beneath contempt." It can reach criminal proportions, as it does for serial killers. If our endowment and experiences in life were the same as theirs, we also might perpetrate such horrors. But, while condemning such actions, it helps to keep an open mind about trying to understand and deal with such people in a human manner (which doesn't mean allowing them to victimize us or others). Who has not, at times, been guilty of disdain, dismissing others' opinions or characteristics rather than trying to understand them?

Exercise 4.7:

Disdain is an emotional protector that is especially difficult to acknowledge because it is overtly damaging to others and therefore painful to admit. The best way to minimize its use is to be alert to when and if you slip into a disdainful attitude. If you do slip, make an apology and, if possible, do something to compensate for whatever damage you have done. Make a list of people, times, and ways you have been disdainful. Make appropriate apologies to all persons on your list who are still available.

Helping Question 4.8:

Are You a Power Seeker?

Ken

Reviewing my life with the help of QUESTIONS helped me realize that as an adolescent, and well into adulthood, I had a powerful need to be a leader—not because I was intent on accomplishing objectives that could only be done from a position of leadership, but because only in the role of leader did I feel safe. This compulsion had a tyrannical power over me that at times shaded into tyranny over others. In high school, thanks to vigorous campaigning, I was elected president of the student council. In college I was more subdued because I had a hard time just surviving. In graduate school, where I prospered academically, I felt free to exercise my compulsion toward leadership once again. I became a leader once more. Devotion to self-promotion once again brought election as president of the student council. I came to know several colleagues who were even more compulsive leaders than me. Their driven and essentially empty lives helped me move toward considering if this was the way I wanted to live.

Over the past ten years, with the help of QUESTIONS my attitude toward leadership has definitely shifted. Coming to realize that an unconscious struggle for power was an important factor in the destruction of my first marriage was critical in convincing me it was past time for me to become fully aware of it and get rid of it.

I now experience leadership as a function among other functions, one no more and no less important than other group functions. I no longer need it to feel secure. I have become, if anything, reluctant to assume leadership positions unless I feel something important is at stake, and there's no one else willing or qualified to take charge. Instead of using conscience as "the inner voice that warns us that someone may be looking," as H. L. Mencken once defined it, I use it as a guide for my own behavior whether others are looking or not.

Exercise 4.8:

There are some things in life that cannot be accomplished without the exercise of power. Seeking power to accomplish something that is justified by its contribution to the common good is worthwhile. What is not worthwhile is seeking power at the expense of others. If that's what a study of your behavior reveals, continuing it will decrease, not increase, your personal happiness.

If you suspect yourself of indiscriminate power-seeking, back off before it is too late! Indiscriminate power-seeking is a very destructive factor in interpersonal and inter group relations. Involve yourself in a review of your values as Angelica, Anthony, Marie, and I do in CENTRAL QUESTION SEVEN: *WHO DO YOU WANT TO BECOME?* and, if that's what you discover, reorder your values in a healthier way. The result will not only end a self-defeating form of behavior, but will increase your ability to contribute to improved interpersonal relationships, as well as improved relationships within local to international groups.

Extra Question 4.8:

Power seeking often disguises itself as unacknowledged competition. Conscious competition, as in sports, can be healthy, but unconscious competition with friends, spouses, or members of your own family is almost always very destructive. Carefully review any relationship in which you suspect it is a factor. Just becoming aware of its presence can be enough for you to end your involvement in it. A complete solution, however, is usually not possible without discussion with the person or persons you are in competition with. Sometimes such discussion is not possible without the help of a therapist. Try first to solve it without such help, but if that doesn't work, don't hesitate to get the help you need.

Helping Question 4.9:

Do Repressed Feelings Interfere With Your Ability to Love and Be Loved?

Marie

After going through QUESTIONS Marie came to understand the powerless position she was in when she was growing up. This led her to become aware that in her current life, she still tends to approach people as though she comes from a powerless position. As she put it, "My assumption, learned as I grew up, is that I have to earn love and have to continue earning it, or it will be withdrawn. So I constantly strive to be loved by being a giving girl, a loving girl, an amusing girl. I rarely relax.

"After I completed QUESTIONS, I reread some of what I read as a young woman on the concept of unconditional love. I rejected that concept as unrealistic the first time I read it. After a second and third reading it made sense to me. I tried it on some of my friends. I gradually learned that I am not powerless. A number of people truly love me, warts and all. I have begun to accept and love myself and others, warts and all."

Freely and generously giving and receiving love is as close as you can get to most human's concept of ideal human interaction. Understanding love and your relation to it, will help you get closer to that ideal.

- Not giving love severely reduces your chances of receiving it, bringing about a "vicious circle" of interaction with others.

- Giving love increases your chances of receiving it, bringing about a "benevolent circle" of interaction with others.

Probably the most serious effect of automatic self-protectiveness, in its various forms, is that it usually affects your ability to love and be loved. Though other factors also affected Marie's abilities along these lines, her chronic aloofness and tendency to blame her partners for problems in her relationships were probably the most decisive. It turned off many a potential lover until she met one who helped her understand its roots. With his help she succeeded, as described in the introduction to CENTRAL QUESTION TWO: *YOUR CHILDHOOD AND ADOLESCENCE: WHAT WAS GOOD, WHAT WAS BAD?*

Exercise 4.9:

Confess what you believe to be your number one repressed feeling to at least one person that you have used it on and ask her/him to let you know if there is any recurrence.

Helping Question 4.10:

Do Repressed Feelings Sometimes Cause You To Violate Your Own Beliefs?

Anthony

"Like most people, by middle age my ways of protecting myself from emotional pain were so integrated into my personality that I was almost completely unaware of them.

"When I began QUESTIONS I considered my ability to express my feelings, and my emotional protectiveness, as about average. In retrospect, I realize that my emotional protectiveness at that time was above average, and my ability to express my feelings was below average. Overall, after going through QUESTIONS, I am now less emotionally protective and more able to express my feelings. Facing unpleasant facts about myself is the price I've gladly paid to get to this more mature place."

Anthony's confrontation of unpleasant facts about himself (his disdain and blaming) conflicted with his own values. Realizing this gave him an extra push toward changing those unpleasant facts. Understanding how emotional self-protectiveness can interfere with your relationships and may be in conflict with your moral code, can give you, too, the extra push you may need to overcome it

Exercise 4.10:

Make a list of your repressed feelings, what you know of their origins, and your program for eliminating them. Share that list with two or three close friends, and make revisions on the basis of their comments.

Extra Mile 4.10:

After a year has past show the list to the friends you showed it to originally and ask them to evaluate your progress.

As with other human attributes, the most important thing is not where you are, but where you are going. Automatic disguises of some feelings are part of the personalities of practically all humans, with the possible exception of saints. Before you have grown up it may be a necessary protection, but after you are an adult it often gets in the way of growth.

Keep a daily diary and analyze it at the end of each of four weeks to identify any nonproductive behavior patterns. At the end of four weeks review your weekly analyses to see what new questions you have raised about your behavior patterns.

In CENTRAL QUESTION FIVE: *HOW'S YOUR LOVE AND SEX LIFE?* we will explore an important area of potential strength in working on reducing the need for protective strategies.

CENTRAL QUESTION FIVE

HOW'S YOUR LOVE AND SEX LIFE?

○ ○

God gave men a brain and a penis, but only enough blood to operate one at a time.

—Woody Allen

Unduly blaming yourself gets in the way of emotional growth. It's the reason I keep emphasizing, ala Newman and Berkowitz, that it's vital to be your own best friend. The quotation that begins this chapter is meant to help you keep focused on this. Being sympathetic and humorous with yourself is certainly not a fault. It can help you benefit from considering your own faults as well as those of others to remember that analysis of mistakes, though often painful, is a vital way to gain insight into yourself and others. The error of always blaming yourself is as bad as the opposite error of always blaming others.

Mr. & Ms. X

My first task when a couple invites me to conduct marital therapy with them is often to determine whether they want to save their marriage, or if one or both want to end it. Mr. and Ms. X began by declaring that they both wanted to save theirs.

After several interviews in which we talked about sex and other matters the word "rape" came to my mind. I couldn't justify it in terms of anything they described. When I shared this association with them, they too couldn't connect with it in any way. I decided it probably reflected a problem of my own that I hoped to clarify at a later time.

After three months of weekly marital therapy sessions, Ms. X announced that she wanted a divorce. We discussed this in depth, then switched from marital to divorce therapy. Divorce therapy lasted about one month, after which they arranged a reasonably amicable parting.

About a year later, Mr. X came back to see me about some personal problems. While working on them he told me that as a preadolescent teenager he had fantasies of running a slave camp of faceless women. As the commandant, he devised all sorts of ways to torture and humiliate the camp's inmates. There was nothing overtly sexual about these tortures and humiliations, though they sometimes involved his urinating on their naked bodies.

After puberty his fantasized inmates acquired the faces of women he knew. He was very ashamed of these fantasies. I was the first person to whom he had ever revealed them. After discussing them in detail we discovered that they were a reaction to his feelings of helplessness with women. As the weeks went by the external power element disappeared. In its place he fantasized becoming a second Rudolph Valentino, acquiring power over women because of his irresistible sexual attractiveness. After further discussion, including discussion of cultural as well as personal factors, this also changed. When his dominant fantasies came to be mutually respectful relationships with women, I knew that our work was over.

After I concluded my individual therapeutic relationship with Mr. X, his former wife also returned for an individual consultation. She was concerned because her post-marital sex life was no more exciting than her marital sex life had been. In the course of discussing this, she told me that while having sex with her former husband (or any other man), she often fantasized that she was in a concentration camp and was being forced to have intercourse with the commandant or one of the guards. This fantasy was necessary for her to reach orgasm.

At last I had the answer to why I sensed "rape" when I worked with these two people as a couple. Their sexual fantasies complemented each other perfectly. When I first saw them, they were caught in an unconscious sexual system which neither would have consciously chosen. Ms. X was aware of her fantasies when having sex but was too embarrassed to reveal them to her husband or to me. Her former husband was aware of having had fantasies in the past, but didn't know that he was acting them out in the present; so he didn't think they were relevant. None of us had been able to correctly assess the unconscious dynamics of their sexual relationship.

An important reason they divorced was that Ms. X felt her husband dominated and abused her, not only in their sex life, but in their everyday life together. For example, while they were in marital therapy with me, she accused him of being cruel and neglectful toward her and their children because he spent most of his time and energy working. He protested that he worked long hours so that she and the children could have a comfortable life. Though there was validity in her anger about her husband's neglect, that anger was magnified by the unconscious anger generated by the regular reenactment of their interlocking sexual fantasies. If we had been able to explore this while they were in therapy together, this unconscious source of some of their marital difficulties might have been resolved. I had unconsciously experienced "vibes" of what was going on sexually, but had no way to confirm them.

They talked to each other after their individual appointments with me about sex in their former marriage. At their request I arranged a joint appointment with them. This didn't result in their remarrying, but did help them in their relationships with their then-current sexual partners; eased some of the pain of their divorce; and contributed to their developing a lasting friendship.

No aspects of human life are more important or more complex than love and sex. As the above example illustrates, there are almost always aspects outside of awareness, which may also be outside the awareness of an "expert."

CENTRAL QUESTION FIVE, *HOW'S YOUR LOVE AND SEX LIFE?* will help you probe and better understand your and your partner's fantasies and basic attitudes regarding love and sex. Improving your love and sex life may be impossible without doing this. It will help you discover any unknown errors and/or deficiencies in yourself and your partner. Love is not love if it can't deal honestly and compassionately with errors and/or deficiencies in ourselves and others.

Helping Question 5.1:

Are You a Sucker for Romance?

Marie

Romantic movies and fiction were a big part of Marie's teenage life. She imagined herself dancing with Fred Astaire, as she walked—or rather, floated—home from the movies. Romantic fantasy was an escape from home, where she was often unhappy. It was also a way to duck the difficulties of growing up sexually.

Marie's first love was Johnny, a high school football star. She had a romantic fantasy about him throughout high school, but they never dated each other. After they both graduated, he called and made a date with her. Most of Marie's energy during their first and only date was expended fighting off his aggressive sexuality. Her romantic dream of a life with him quickly faded.

In college, Marie frequently had someone to fantasize about, but real romance passed her by until her last year, when she fell in love with Arthur. He insisted that sex should be a part of their relationship. She refused, and he left her.

She moved to California where she met Bert, with whom she had a wild, tempestuous, romance that included sex only when they were both drunk. It ended after four months, on his initiative. It left her with years of obsessive thoughts about their brief but very traumatic relationship.

After seven years she met Carl and once more fell in love. This time "in love" was combined with "loving." She had met a person who loved and understood her in a way she had never experienced. Out of consideration for her fear of sex, he agreed to no sex until they were married.

Their relationship has had its ups and downs, but is much better than her relationship with Arthur or Bert ever was, and, in addition, gets better year by year.

All human emotions are subject to distortion, manipulation and hypocrisy. Also, fashions and modes of expressing emotions vary from family to family, culture to culture, and generation to generation. One of the most common sources of difficulty is confusion over what constitutes "love."

I make a distinction between "loving" and being "in love." Loving implies that the lover genuinely knows, and freely and affectionately accepts, the loved one, warts and all. Being in love is generally a more temporary state, something like being in heat. It implies that the lover does not truly know or accept all of the qualities of the loved one, but only their positive qualities, which may be exaggerated. As comedian Henny Youngman commented, "My wife and I were happy for twenty years. Then we met."

Being in love is primarily romantic. Loving often includes romance, but may not, as in India, where men like to say, "you Americans fall in love and then marry, we Indians marry and then fall in love." Both cultural modes have their advantages and disadvantages. I have worked professionally only with American marriages and have found that many of them have been improved by considering the Indian model after having married using the American model

Anthony

Anthony first fell in love in the third grade. Her name was Irene, and she was the prettiest girl in the class. At that time the song "Good Night Irene" was popular. Though only eight years old, he identified completely with the lyrics. He still remembers singing, "Good Night Irene, Good Night Irene, I'll see you in my dreams!" before going to sleep. He was crushed when at a show-and-tell gathering of eight-year-olds, Irene shyly confided that she was in love with another boy.

After one year of being in love with Irene, Anthony moved with his family to another neighborhood on the opposite side of the city. He quickly forgot Irene and fell in love with Helen, the prettiest girl in his new neighborhood. He remained in love with Helen until he entered high school, where he fell in love with Penny, the prettiest girl in the tenth grade.

When he was about to graduate from high school, Anthony agonized for days before asking Penny to the senior prom. To his great gratification, when he asked her, she accepted. His hopes leaped. For the next two weeks he was lost in endless fantasies of their future life together. After the prom he went through further agonies before he finally kissed her good night. It was the first time he kissed a girl when it wasn't part of a kissing game. For the next two years she was the center of his thoughts, though she let him know she wasn't interested in going any further with their "romance."

During the ensuing years a number of girls expressed a romantic interest in him, but Anthony found it impossible to respond. His experience with Penny had been crushing. He wasn't able to kiss a girl for two years after that first and last good night kiss. That didn't inhibit his powerful sex drive, however. If anything, his sex drive became more powerful and finally prevailed. He forced himself to kiss a girl. After that, it was relatively easy, but he did it without any emotion that resembled love. As a result of his painful experiences with "love," he adopted the Victorian belief that love and sex are incompatible. He conditioned himself to concentrate on sex without love. This resulted in a number of brief sexual relationships. He was dissatisfied with their brevity, and his partners were dissatisfied with the absence of love.

Being in love is powerful. The physical and psychological connection can be very strong. For most people in the U.S. it is essential for starting a long term love relationship. At its best, being in love will change into loving as romance matures over a period of time. Assessing where you are regarding loving and being in love, and planning how you can move more strongly in the direction of loving, makes this more likely.

Exercise 5.1:

Reflect on your current romance or marriage with special attention to what happened to the feeling of love that probably propelled you into it in the first place.

- Imagine your current romance as a romantic movie. What must you and your partner overcome for it to have a "happy ending."
- Perhaps, like Marie, you confused being in love with loving. Or, like Anthony, you remain traumatized, afraid to allow yourself to be fully committed to a member of the opposite sex. Do either of these situations apply to you? If so, devise a plan, with the help of your lover or spouse, for working through these issues.

Extra Mile 5.1:

It is also possible that there is a fundamental difference in values between you and your lover or spouse. Perhaps you overlooked such difference at the time you first got together or perhaps it developed in the course of your relationship. If you suspect that your problem is of this kind, I urge you to consider a couples counselor. It is unlikely to be resolved without such help.

Helping Question 5.2:

What Were Your First, and What Are Your Current Sexual Fantasies?

Mark

In the latter half of the tenth grade, my client Mark attended an assembly for boys only. The school doctor gave a sex lecture. Mark didn't know what the doctor was talking about, but he gathered it had something to do with the erections he had been having for some time. The doctor's advice was that exercise would reduce their strength and frequency. After the school doctor's talk, the school nurse added a short but pithy postscript. Mark still remembers her exact words: "If I catch any of you weeds of boys hurting my flowers of girls, you'll have me to answer to!"

"This is confusing!," Mark thought. "I'm a weed? Girls are flowers? The school nurse is afraid I'm going to hurt them? I am in love with one of those flowers! I don't think of sex with her. I don't even want to see her naked—that's for older women with big tits!"

While growing up, Mark learned nothing about sex through open and reciprocal communication. An example of this strangulated communication was a sharp reprimand he received from his father for exciting a dog's penis with a stick when he was twelve years old. No explanation came with the reprimand. His motive was curiosity regarding his accidental discovery that rubbing what he thought was part of the dog's belly caused a red cylinder of flesh to emerge between the dog's rear legs. He vaguely knew that what the dog had between his legs was another version of what he had between his. The message he received was that it was sinful to stimulate "that thing," and even to be curious about it. As a result, he put off any contact with his penis as long as he could. This made it all the more difficult for him when he finally began to masturbate.

He didn't yield to sexually pleasuring himself until he was in college, but once started, he made up for lost time. Masturbation became an irresistible compulsion, a nightly temptation. He would resist for three or four nights, followed by an orgy of self-gratification, followed by waves of guilt and the resolution never to do it again—a resolution that lasted three or four days and was followed by another orgy and another resolution. In spite of reading and hearing that masturbation was normal and natural, even beneficial, his guilt remained unaffected. He had absorbed it from the culture in which he was brought up. His experience with the dog is an example of the indirect way in which his culture transmitted a message different from the one he read about.

Mark's adolescent sexual fantasies revolved around seeing women naked. One of his favorites when he was in high school involved him and his Latin teacher. His Latin teacher happened to be physically well endowed. In a recurring dream she secretly entered Mark's bedroom, undressed, and showed him all her sexual charms. If that had actually happened, he told me, he wouldn't have known what to do except to stare.

In the eleventh grade a girl in Mark's class invited him to her house ostensibly to help her do her homework. On arrival he was invited to sit next to her on the living room sofa. She started their conversation by asking "Would you like to see me in a bathing suit?" Before he could answer she left the room and quickly reappeared wearing one of the more daring bathing suits of that day. He was speechless and paralyzed. She left again and quickly returned fully dressed. They started on her homework. This was the closest he had ever come to realizing his fantasy of seeing a naked, fully developed woman. Instead of feeling gratified, however, he only felt scared. He left as soon as he could.

After he started masturbating his fantasies took on a more aggressive character. In his new fantasies he was transformed into a man who radiated irresistible sexual attractiveness. He only needed to crook his finger to capture the eager compliance of any woman he chose, and he chose dozens. Women he saw in the movies, on the sidewalks, or in faculty offices were all candidates. After about a year of this, he made some tentative sexual approaches, the most daring of which was to feel the breasts of two girls. Rejection of these cautious forays sobered him considerably. He began to see himself as a frightened, ineffectual, dirty-minded boy.

His first sexual intercourse occurred with a prostitute. He was 18 years old and didn't have the courage to initiate it. The prostitute showed him the way. "You wanna suck?" "You wanna fuck?" All he had to do was nod. As Mark put it:

"I didn't know how to begin; she showed me. Not the ideal way to begin a healthy/normal sex life, but at least a start. That start gave me the courage to initiate a sexual relationship with a woman I fell in love with at a sophomore dance. It was my first true love affair. It was a gateway to a whole new realm of being. Through sex I experienced and expressed tenderness, love, and intimacy; feelings that I experienced before only in a general, unfocused way. I discovered a new language and access to a new world."

Though sex was his route to intimacy, in retrospect, Mark realized it was also an unconscious vehicle to express his power needs, which were of the male-macho variety very common at the time. Looking back, he was astonished to realize that in his first serious adult love affair he unconsciously acted out a need to dominate. This mostly took the form of denigrating the woman he was in love with. He would, for example, make fun of her ignorance about mechanical gadgets and sneer at her naiveté regarding sex. He wanted sex as an expression of love, but used it as an expression of dominance. This was an important reason their love affair ended. It would be five years before he could again combine love and sex in one relationship—with a woman who soon became his wife.

The unconscious need to dominate in a love relationship, though tempered by reflection, continued in his marriage. It took the form of irrational annoyance whenever his wife disagreed with him. It made a substantial contribution to their eventual divorce.

Exercise 5.2:

Review the evolution of your sexual fantasies, defining your current fantasies as precisely as you can. Are your beliefs and your fantasies congruent? If not, like Mark, decide which (perhaps both) should be changed so they will become congruent. Act upon the changes you want to make and evaluate the results.

Helping Question 5.3:

What, For You, Is the Ideal Relationship Between Love and Sex??

Angelica

Angelica's family and the society she was brought up in condemned extramarital sex, so she avoided it. At the age of eighteen, however, her sexual feelings caused her to violate that boundary. She had intercourse with a boyfriend followed by severe guilt. The experience stiffened her resolve. From then on, though still flirtatious, she always managed to withhold intercourse. She went through a series of engagements until she met her first husband-to-be, Ted, with whom she had her next experience with intercourse. Her guilt, however, prevented her from enjoying it. They were soon married and had an active sex life that Ted enjoyed and Angelica tolerated. Sexual resentments piled up in Angelica's mind, but she could not communicate them to Ted. Those resentments, Angelica's inability to communicate them verbally, combined with Ted's inability to translate her non-verbal communication of them, had a decisive influence in bringing their marriage to an end.

Angelica never heard her parents say they loved each other or found each other sexually attractive. Her attitudes toward love and sex were the same as theirs, conveyed non-verbally, as her parents conveyed theirs. Even after her second marriage (to Anthony) her concept of sex remained "a necessary evil." For Anthony it remained "something to be enjoyed separate from love."

As they interacted together in a more open and honest way, both of these concepts gradually changed. By fits and starts, and some reversals, they began to respond to each other freely in loving sex. They have now grown to a place where sex is a nourishing way in which they give and receive love.

Most people of Anthony's, Angelica's, Mark's, Marie's, and my generation were trained, as were the Victorians, to think of love and sex as incompatible with each other. This made their integration in a single relationship, which is the ideal of most religious and mental health groups, very difficult. The present generation, by reducing guilt about sexuality, has moved closer to this ideal. Some however, have another problem: sex without love or guilt, bringing with it an explosion of disease and teen-age pregnancy. As Lily Tomlin said, "I worry about kids today. Because of the sexual revolution, they're going to grow up and never know what 'dirty' means."

I view the energy of raw sex in the same way that I view the energy of raw anger and fear. It can be expressed in ways that are extraordinarily destructive. It is, however, a vital raw material for building communion and love. For that to happen, the raw energy of sex must be transmuted into the compassionate energy of communion and love. Training in Marshall Rosenberg's nonviolent communication (NVC) can be a big help.

When clients struggle to formulate their goals about love and sex, I recommend they consider the integration of the two, a goal that some never considered. I see such an integration as a vital step in becoming fully human: converting the raw animal reality of hormones into an expression of love. Freud called this "sublimation" and took the position that sex was the paramount human drive. I believe that whichever is paramount, love or sex, varies from person to person according to his or her genetic endowment, life circumstances, beliefs, and emotional maturity.

Combining all of the above concepts is a genuinely creative act that is unlikely to happen unless both partners believe in it and consciously strive to attain it. In our society it seems to be easier for women than for men to subscribe to and practice these ideals. As Woody Allen said, "God gave males a penis and a brain, but only enough blood to operate one at a time," while Billy Crystal said, "A woman needs a reason to make love, a man needs a place."

The dictionary defines compassion as "sympathetic consciousness of other's distress and a desire to alleviate it." This along with empathy, which implies a power to enter into and understand another's emotional experiences, is vital to the establishment of good human relationships. These two qualities were present in all of the successful human relationships cited in this book and absent in those that were not successful.

The energy of anger, fear and hurt can be combined with the energy of understanding and compassion. To do this, it is vital that you dig into the deepest parts of yourself, as QUESTIONS will help you do, until you get to what connects all human beings. If you go deep into yourself, you will make contact with the underground river that connects all of nature. You can then act in terms of what is best for you, blended with what is best for the universe of which we are all a part. In the process you will come to know that happiness cannot be found by following false premises, such as that the acquisition of wealth and fame will lead to happiness. The Royal Road to happiness will be found when you turn your energies toward those things that you know in your bones will be more happiness-yielding for you. This often takes a lot of living. Anthony and Angelica didn't achieve it until they were both in their fifties.

Exercise 5.3:

Review your parents' and your peers' attitudes toward love and sex when you were growing up. What were yours? What are they now?

- Does your behavior correspond to your ideals? Do you share your attitudes and ideals with your love/sex partner?

- Write down three memorable sexual discoveries or experiences. What can you can you learn from them now?

- If your responses to any of these questions is unsatisfactory to you, formulate a plan for changing them in the direction you desire. Practice those changes until they become a part of you.

Helping Question 5.4:

What Were the Prescribed Love and Sex Roles When You Were Growing Up?

Gender Differences

As the psychiatrist in T. S. Eliot's play The Cocktail Party says, "People are all different, and very much like each other."

When it comes to sex, however, the current differences between men and women are clear. Early in a sexual relationship men usually want more sex than women. Later, the balance sometimes shifts in the other direction. To put it another way: "Why do so many women fake orgasms?" Answer: "Because so many men fake foreplay."

Gender differences are undoubtedly influenced by hormones and heredity as well as by culturally-prescribed gender roles. Many of my male friends and I went through early adulthood seeking confirmation as males by having sexual intercourse as early and as often as possible. Although hormones played a major role, social pressure also played a significant, and sometimes dominant role.

Nina

I met Nina at San Diego State University when we were both students in a women's' studies course. She was nineteen, I was sixty nine. One day after class, she asked me if she could talk with me. We met in the cafeteria. She told me that she had heard I was a psychologist. After considerable beating around the bush, she told me that she was troubled by her sexual promiscuity. She couldn't refuse any sexual offer, though she knew she would curse herself afterward, and wanted my advice as to what she could do about it. I gave her a draft of this chapter.

The next week she came back all aglow, telling me she had finally solved her problem! Her response to "How did your parents' personalities affect you?" gave her the key. Her mother and her grandmother both were beauty queens when they were young. Nina admired her mother and grandmother, both of whom were convinced that physical beauty was essential for establishing good relationships with men. Nina bought into this belief, but she was not a beauty, so she chose the next best means of attracting men: sexual availability. Once she realized the origin of her sexual compulsion she renounced it and told me she was cured. I've had many professional experiences with people who think they are cured after one blinding insight, but who later find it takes more than that to solve a deep and long-term problem. I urged her to put her newfound insight into practice and continue with the study of her life. I gave her a draft of the entire manuscript of QUESTIONS to help her in that endeavor. We met weekly after that for a cup of coffee and discussion until the end of the semester. She discovered that insight, though vital, is only the beginning of real change. By responding to the questions in the preceding and remaining chapters, and practicing new ways of relating to her mother and grandmother, she discovered other significant areas where their influence had been less than healthy. This, along with deliberately changing the dependent nature of her relationship with them, as well as with others, put a solid foundation under her initial insight. She still had to make a considerable number of trials before it resulted in a lasting solution to her problem with sexual promiscuity and a better understanding and enjoyment of her life as a whole. One-trial learning is rare, though possible. If you, like Nina, don't solve a problem on the first trial, don't give up, repeated trials will reveal other dimensions, which when taken into account, will result in a solution.

I recently learned that Nina had married and is the mother of a baby girl. I'm sure what she teaches her daughter about physical beauty will be more enlightened than what she was taught.

Exercise 5.4:

Before they completed responding to CENTRAL QUESTION FIVE, HOW'S YOUR LOVE AND SEX LIFE?, many of the people whose lives we have touched on in this book were not fully aware of how their early training in love and sex affected their later behavior. Review your responses to this question up to this point. If any part of what was true of Angelica, Anthony, Marie, Mark, me, and Nina is true for you, use the methods they used to decide which part of your early training in love and sex is no longer acceptable to you, and make a note of it. Begin a program designed to change your behavior in those areas. Evaluate your progress periodically until you are convinced that you have made the changes you want to make.

Helping Question 5.5:

How Do Gender Stereotypes Affect the Way You Conduct Yourself as a Lover?

Anthony

Like most men of the last generation, Anthony was unaware of gender role indoctrination as he was growing up. He was only aware that women were beyond his understanding, though he was powerfully attracted to them. Consciously, he considered girls and women superior to boys and men—"made of finer stuff"—as his father was fond of saying. At the same time he regarded his younger sister as generally inferior. That's also the way she regarded herself, which didn't help. Given these contradictions, no wonder he had difficulties when the time came to establish an intimate relationship with a woman other than his sister or his mother.

The first experience Anthony had where being male was a crucial factor happened at age nineteen. He lived in Manhattan, his girlfriend lived in Queens. One evening he picked her up in his family's car and they drove to a theater in Manhattan. After the play, he suggested they drive to the nearest subway stop so she could take the train back to Queens. She told him this was unacceptable. He was a man; he had to drive her home. He felt trapped by his girlfriend's demand, especially since she implied it was a general social demand. To his surprise he found himself sobbing all the way to Queens.

In retrospect, he realized that his sobbing was due to his feeling that it was outrageous that he should drive an extra forty miles through stop-and-go New York City traffic when his girlfriend could return home by subway and be home quicker and more safely than if he drove her. All his accumulated feelings of being under the control of women, while being expected to take care of them, broke through. He wanted to be loved by women, but the price was too high. The experience of gender behavioral expectations plus the repressed hurt from his mother's on-and-off physical abuse when he was a child was the source of his agony at that time. (His mother's on and off physical abuse was outlined in his responses to CENTRAL QUESTION THREE, *HOW DO YOU HANDLE ANGER, FEAR, SADNESS?*)

Gender Prejudice has played a part in the personality formation of almost every woman brought up in the American culture. The same goes for men, though they are generally less aware of the ways sexism has determined their attitudes.

Many women continue to be abused in our society by men who often don't realize that they are being abusive. Some women have such deeply repressed awareness of the abuse they've experienced they can only recall it with the help of psychotherapy. Those who haven't been sexually or physically abused have nevertheless usually suffered from sexism to some degree.

I've worked with many women who feel their needs take second place to those of men. I have worked with men who feel that they have to pursue soul-deadening careers in order to support their families. I have worked with angry women who could only relate to men as enemies. I have worked with men who felt they had to be dominant in any heterosexual relationship. The list goes on and on. This is an area of life that affects everyone.

In the last two decades a great deal has been learned about the enormous impact of sexism on the lives of both men and women. Overtly, it has had a much greater and more obvious impact on women than on men. In addition to becoming aware of the great injustice that women have suffered because of it, men are just beginning to realize that they too suffer. Any advantage they may seem to get from dominating women is much less than the problems of women's resentment (and often covert retaliation) that it creates.

Helping Question 5.6

How, If At All, Did Falling in Love Change Your Concepts of Love and Sex?

Earl is a member of a group of older men. They have been meeting once a month for about five years. They meet in each others houses and discuss any topic that they agree to discuss. Last year Earl brought up a topic that had been bothering him for the last fifty years.

At age twenty four he returned to college after spending three years in the army, years during which he believes that he grew up considerably. He rose in rank from private to first lieutenant, had sexual experiences with several women, including living with a German woman for six months after World War II. He had been "in love" twice before the war. He never kissed the first girl he was in love with, and kissed the second only in a game of spin-the-bottle. Upon his return from overseas, after being in college for three months, he fell madly in love with Delia, a nineteen year old coed. They had sex (she for the first time) after which she returned his love. They planned to marry and go to graduate school together. He, however, had some doubts as to whether his intended was really ready to marry, and suggested that they not see each other over the summer so she could take that time to make sure she was ready for such a big step. After the summer he received a "Dear John" letter from her telling him that she wanted to explore other relationships. He saw her several times over the next five years, all on his initiative. It was clear that she no longer had any romantic interest in him. Both of them became interested in other people, have been married (he's on his second marriage) and raised families. His problem is that he has never been able to get his first great love out of his mind, though they haven't as much as seen each other for the last forty years.

Earl discussed this problem with his group and got some good advice from its members. He then consulted with me and we went through most of QUESTIONS together. He discovered that because of his early experiences in his family of origin, he really never felt loved. He did feel loved by Delia, who he regarded as a Goddess. As undergraduates, he was a below average student, while she was an above average student. Unconsciously, as an undergraduate he felt like she was his salvation. He subsequently was an outstanding Ph.D. student, but that didn't affect his unconscious feeling that she was superior to him. She came from a very class conscious family and always regarded herself as being his social superior. He agreed with her though he believed that the whole concept of confining relationships by class is wrong. He realized, comparing his self-analysis with his analysis of her, that marriage between them would have resulted in disaster. He is now married to a lovely lady who is not class conscious. They have developed a better relationship than he could ever have developed with Delia. He thought (perhaps with some justification) that the reason Delia originally fell in love with him was due to him being the first man she ever had sex with. On the other hand it was the first time Earl had sex with someone he loved, and that was very special for him. It was the beginning of a total revision of his concept of sex as a way of expressing love, not just getting his rocks off.

Earl will never forget his relationship with Delia, but his thoughts and feelings about her are pleasant and no longer a source of frustration.

Exercise 5.6

Trace the development of your concepts of love and sex. Have they changed over the years? Have you succeeded in considering and experiencing, sex as an expression of love? If not, would you like to experience it in this way? What interferes? If you discover what interferes what are you going to do to about it?

Helping Question 5.7:

How is the Mesh Between Your Role and the Role of Your Lover?

Angelica

In Angelica's relationship with her first husband, she continued playing the role of family healer that she played opposite her younger sister in her family of origin. In the course of that marriage she finally abandoned the role of healer. A healthy development. Her husband, however, experienced this change as a betrayal of her unspoken pledge to devote herself to healing him. Her resignation from this role, along with his refusal to seek professional help, were important factors in bringing about their eventual separation and divorce.

Joseph

My client Joseph expected to star in the role of father. His college work had included courses in child psychology. To his dismay, he found that taking a couple of courses didn't help much. He dealt with his children, especially his son, Jimmy, much as his stepfather had dealt with him. When he was a teenager, one of his stepfather's favorite derisive questions was, "How old are you, Joseph?," implying that it was unbelievable that someone of Joseph's advanced years could act in such infantile ways.

Joseph didn't ask Jimmy how old he was. He was more brutal and "honest" in condemning him as he had been condemned. He didn't consider the devastating effect of his harshness on his son's self-esteem, as his stepfather hadn't considered the effects of his sarcastic question on him. At one point, Jimmy bought a used motorcycle, drove it without a license while drunk, and was arrested. Jimmy's only response to Joseph's outrage was to look at him helplessly. Completely out of control, Joseph shouted, "You look like a bag of shit!" Afterwards Joseph's former wife told him that Jimmy shuddered when he said that. For the first time, Joseph got a glimmer of insight into the destructiveness of his explosive anger.

Psychological research clearly shows that the person we experience as the authority in our family of origin is the person we are most likely to use as a model for our own behavior. Joseph patterned himself after his stepfather, the authority in his family of origin, and his son Jimmy patterned himself after Joseph, the authority in Jimmy's family of origin. Joseph's stepfather was a part-time tyrant, but he wasn't a bad father. Like Joseph, he was well-intentioned, but when upset, treated Joseph harshly, the way he was treated by his father. When Jimmy was upset he repeated this generation-to-generation cycle with his son.

Exercise 5.7:

- Review the work you did on understanding your family background when responding to Central Questions One and Two. Can you recognize similarities between the way your father treated his wife and the way you and your spouse interact? Decide which of those similarities you want to retain and which want to change. Work on those you want to change.

- If you are unmarried, but intend to marry eventually, train yourself to treat the important woman or man in your life the way you wish your mother and father had treated each other

Extra Mile 5.7:

If you have children, or are looking forward to having them in the future, train yourself to treat them the way you wish you had been treated as a child. Devise better responses to situations that hurt you long ago. Practice replaying those scenes using the revised script you have devised (with an understanding friend perhaps). If, in the course of everyday interaction, you lose your temper with your child or spouse, apologize and play that scene over again. Play over any scene that you're dissatisfied with. Eventually this training will pay off, and you'll find it less and less necessary to apologize or play scenes over.

Good human relationships generally depend on wisdom and understanding, which can best be found through probing our own nature. This leads to the keys—love and compassion—we need for understanding ourselves and others. PART THREE, *HOW EMOTIONALLY MATURE ARE YOU?* Will help you answer this important question, after which CENTRAL QUESTION SIX, *WHO ARE YOU?* will lead you to a consideration of self-protective behavior that may have been useful when you were growing up but which in adulthood often interferes with developing and realizing the love and compassion essential to finding the best that is in you and others.

PART III

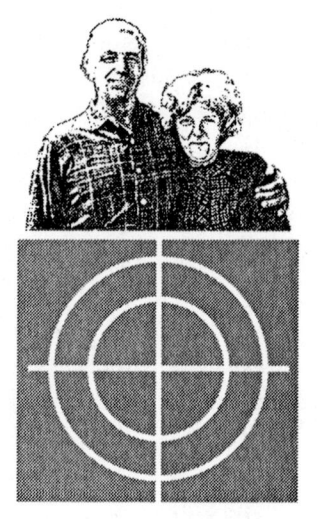

How Emotionally Mature Are You?

○ ○
*The best way to change how people treat you
is to change how you treat them.*

—*Sam Horn*

We all know that there are factors that can interfere with normal emotional growth, often outside of the awareness of the person who has experienced such interference. In Part One we traced your early history to try to identify factors that might have done this to you. Part Two addressed specific symptoms that presently may be interfering with your emotional growth. Having prepared yourself in these ways, you are now ready to address the question "where am I in regard to emotional growth?"

One way of measuring your degree of emotional maturity is the degree you are aware of your emotions and able to choose how you respond to them. The steps in attaining individual emotional maturity are essentially the same as those that apply to societies and groups. In addition to this, humans and human societies have been evolving for about 70,000 years. Being aware of these two facts, individuals and societies can, with hard work, choose not to act on tendencies that are no longer appropriate.

We have arrived at an unprecedented time in human history. Achieving fuller awareness of ourselves is more possible than it has ever been in the past, and can help us improve, maintain, and even surpass ourselves as never before. In addition to personal gain, if we join others who have achieved fuller self-awareness we can help co-create an emotionally mature *nation*, which can inspire other nations and produce an emotionally mature *world*.

Every human resembles every other human and yet is different from every other human. There are different approaches to understanding humans, all of which have validity, but have different degrees of validity for each individual. Current major approaches are through philosophy, mythology, physiology, politics, sociology, psychology, spirituality, science, religion, and common sense. It is desirable that all humans have some grounding in each of these approaches and try especially to make an effort to integrate their understandings in terms of their personal values. This is similar to understanding the different organs of the human body and how they can best all cooperate with each other for the best functioning of the whole.

The approach to self-understanding that is focused on in this book is psychological. Within psychological, as within other approaches, there are differences in what is emphasized. The emphasis in this book is on growing toward emotional maturity through the use of a psychological approach which emphasizes the concept that emotional problems are created and maintained in social, cultural, and political contexts.

CENTRAL QUESTION SIX

WHO ARE YOU?

o o o o o o o o o o o o o o o o o o o o o o o o o o o o o o
Everyone wants to be Cary Grant
I want to be Cary Grant too.

—Cary Grant

I had my first experience with a certifiably mentally ill person when I was twelve years old. My mother and I visited her friend Martha, whose twenty six year old daughter, Rose, had recently been released from a mental hospital. My mother and Martha decided to go out for lunch. They left me with Rose. As they left, I overheard Martha reassuring my mother that it wouldn't harm me to be alone with Rose.

As soon as they left, Rose showed me a collection of household objects that she had carefully arranged on a card table. They were mostly in pairs that were similar but not identical: two toy soldiers, two bottle caps, two needles, two photographs, and several others that I no longer remember. A few things were unpaired; a small scissors, an ashtray, a comic book. Rose said, "I'm trying to put together things that belong together. Will you help me find things that belong with this scissors, ashtray, and comic book?"

She and I searched through the apartment looking for suitable mates for these unpaired items. We found a small dish that we paired with the ashtray, an illustrated paper back book that we paired with the comic book, and a knife that we paired with the scissors. We were both pleased with the results of our search. Rose then put more items on the card table and suggested that we look for what went with them. By that time I had lost interest in the matching game and replied: "How about we read the comic book?" She O.K.'d this idea and listened while I read.

I later learned from my mother that Rose had spent the last three months playing her matching game with anyone who would play it with her. She would play it for hours if the other person didn't break it off. It took me twenty years to make an informed guess as to the meaning of Rose's preoccupation.

We all need a sense of ourselves as separate persons as well as a sense of belonging to some human group. When we start our lives our first sense of personal identity is that we are the children of our parents. We never lose that sense of our identity, but it becomes one of many others, some of which are hopefully stronger that the original.

At the time I visited Rose I believe she was searching for who she was. She was doing it by searching for where she belonged. Did she belong where she was or did she belong back in the mental hospital? She didn't know, nor did I. I hope that later in her life she became aware of what she was really searching for, found it, and has gone on from there.

The quote on the title page for this question succinctly expresses an important quality about who we are as human beings: we tend for both biological and cultural reasons to want to be liked by the important people in our lives.. This is as true about our relationships with groups as it is about our relationships with individuals and with ourselves. I don't believe (as most Buddhists do) that we are born over and over until we achieve enlightenment, but I do believe that we all have the opportunity to live many lives within a single lifetime. If we have no insight into our "earlier" lives, "later" lives tend to be tediously repetitive. One of the important challenges of life is confronting ingrained patterns which result in boredom, dissatisfaction, failure, and sometimes tragedy. With insight (a measure of enlightenment) our lives tend to be progressively more exciting, satisfying, successful, and gratifying.

We are social creatures. Belonging to human groups is vital to our survival and growth. CENTRAL QUESTION SIX: *WHO ARE YOU?*, will help you trace the development of your feelings of who you are and where you belong. You will be encouraged to evaluate where you are currently, and how you got there. The next (and last) Central Question: *WHO DO YOU WANT TO BECOME?* will help you trace the development of your feelings about where you'd like to be in the future. Character sketches in this and the next chapter will illustrate how some people turned from ineffective to effective ways of discovering who they are and where they belong.

To meet the interpersonal demands of life we all play roles. The way we play them is influenced by how our role models play them plus our own beliefs. CENTRAL QUESTION SIX, *WHO ARE YOU?*, will help you become aware of:

- The role models you have been exposed to and how you feel about them.
- The roles you are presently playing and whether they reflect your true self.
- What changes (if any) you would like to make.

A man or woman who was neglected as a child and has repressed their memory of it, becomes a neglectful parent. Another man or woman who was also neglected as a child but remembers it keenly, learns new skills, and becomes an especially loving considerate parent. *Being aware of what happened to you and how you reacted to it can make all the difference.*

Angelica

As she was growing up, Angelica's mother always yielded to her husband. Their marriage could be described as a master-slave relationship where both parties accepted the arrangement. Angelica viewed this as the normal relationship between husbands and wives, with its unspoken assumption that wives and daughters always play second fiddle to husbands and fathers. She felt that she would lose a man's love if she were to challenge this assumption. At that time and place she was right.

When she married, Angelica graduated from playing second fiddle to her father to playing second fiddle to her husband, John. She believed this was necessary to keep John's love. At that time and place she was right.

After reviewing her emotional autobiography, Angelica became angry over the unspoken rules governing her marriage. She resolved to stop playing 'one down', whatever the cost. Her attempt to do so was interpreted by John as a lack of respect for him and resulted in a separation, initiated by him. After three months he returned, saying he was willing to work toward resolving their differences. Their reunion lasted for two months, after which Angelica initiated a second separation which resulted in divorce a year later.

Helping Question 6.1:

What Are Your Current Life Roles?

We all play roles in life. Playing a role does not mean that a person is not being real. He or she is not being real only if they play one or more roles in ways that do not reflect who they really are. I chose the quotation from Cary Grant, a popular American movie star when I was growing up, to dramatize a question that everyone trying to answer the question WHO AM I? should ask themselves. It dramatizes the often startling differences between the roles we play, and the ways we play them, and the persons we really are or want to become. Cary Grant played roles for a living. There's nothing wrong with that. It happened that the central role he played was one he would like to feel really was him. I suspect that playing it probably helped him to move, to some degree, toward being that kind of a person. There is a thin line between compliance and adaptability. It is so thin that we all violate it at times. Practicing with the intention of trying to be who we would like to become can help us actually become who we would like to be.

Exercise 6.1:

Make a list of the roles you have played, and how you played them. Compare them to those you currently play and how you play them. Specify how you learned both, how they have affected your particular growth and development, and whether they reflect who you really were/are. Acknowledge who you really are while practicing who you would like to become.

According to George Burns, "Acting is all about honesty. If you can fake that, you've got it made." Some people apply George Burns' advice to playing roles in everyday life, and experience disaster rather than having it made.

Helping Question 6.2:

Are You Comfortable With Your Current Life Roles?

Hannah Green

In her book *I Never Promised You a Rose Garden*, Hannah Green (a pseudonym) describes a fictional woman (based on the life of a real woman) whose recovery from mental illness began when she found herself on the back ward of a mental hospital. There, at last, she found a role she knew she could play, that of a crazy person. For the first time in her life she felt fully accepted and genuine.

Joan, a client of mine, had a similar experience when she was a teenager. She was brought up in a Hasidic Jewish family, a culture in which women are carefully segregated from men and were expected to defer to them. The Hasidim, when she was a child, lived in a virtual ghetto separating them not only from non-Jews, but also from *non-Hasidic* Jews. Still, as in the film *The Chosen*, referred to earlier, elements of American culture filtered through to her, especially after she and a non-Hasidic Jewish girl became friends.

As a teenager Joan fell in love with a non-Jewish boy. Under pressure from her parents, she gave him up and married the Hasidic man to whom she was betrothed at an early age. She tried playing the role of a traditional Hasidic wife and became severely depressed. In a mental hospital, feeling she had nothing to lose, she let herself be herself, freely expressing all her mixed up, contradictory, and confused feelings. To her surprise she found that she was accepted nonetheless and welcomed into the company of patients and therapists. This accepting atmosphere encouraged her to define the conflict between what she wanted and what her parents wanted of her. That was the beginning of her recovery. She is now a successful social worker married to a Reform Jewish Rabbi. She is reconciled with her parents and, more importantly, with herself. Her life is an inspiration to all who know her.

Another client's parents assigned her the role of helping their relationship go smoothly. No small job, given the level of frustration of her intelligent and assertive mother and the explosiveness of her loving but narcissistic father. Fortunately, she was a natural for the job. She intuitively used her playful, cheerful, personality to play the role of conciliator. She often defused the explosive encounters between them, and later helped her older brother resolve the tensions he suffered because of their father's expectations. Their father expected male members of the family to enter the family jewelry business, but her brother refused to do so. She managed to get them to compromise. Her brother became a marketing specialist with the family business as his first account. She became affectionately known as the family social worker.

Exercise 6.2

From the list of formal and informal roles you made in Exercise 6.1 select the roles you are presently playing. Circle the troublesome ones in red. Specify what, if any, changes you plan to make in the roles circled in red. Practice acting on the changes you have decided to make until they become automatic

Helping Question 6.3:

Did You Ever Try To Buy Or Steal Love?

Angelica

As a little girl, every morning, before her father awoke, Angelica stole whatever loose change he had in the pockets of his trousers. Her daily "take" made her the most affluent pupil in her second-grade class. She treated her classmates to ice cream, candy, and other goodies, symbolically buying their love—while symbolically stealing love from her father.

One day her teacher urged the class to buy and plant saplings which were available at cost through a local group dedicated to the greening of the community. Little Miss Big Spender Angelica bought a dozen—more than any other member of the class. On the last day of the school year the custodian found a dozen dried up saplings in her locker. Her teacher gave her a dressing down in class, accusing her of being extravagant and wasteful. Her classmates chimed in, telling the teacher that Angelica spent a lot of money buying them candy and other things.

To paraphrase H. L. Mencken, conscience is sometimes the inner voice that warns us that someone may be looking. The incident in her second grade class didn't stop Angelica's stealing, but did teach her to be more careful about how she did it and what she did with the proceeds.

As an adult Angelica unconsciously repeated her pattern of trying to steal love. She didn't feel good about making passes at her friends' lovers, but felt compelled to do so. Trying to understand this compulsion brought her face to face with her childhood compulsion to steal change from her father's pockets. She realized for the first time that both were attempts to steal what she believed she could get in no other way. This led to coming to grips with her feeling that she was unlovable and therefore had to steal love. There was no other way!

It is true that Angelicas' parents' love was imperfect (whose isn't?), but in reviewing her life she came to see that this did not make her unlovable. Relief from this burden allowed her to seek love in more realistic ways. She realized as an adult that she is definitely lovable, and is, in fact, currently loved by her husband, her two children, and one special friend. This insight helped her get over her love-stealing compulsion. She now accepts love gratefully when it comes her way and doesn't quibble if it's imperfect (which it almost always is to some degree). Her two children don't steal change from their father's trousers; they get an ample and clearly evident supply of love from both parents.

Exercise 6.3:

Play the role of Disk Jockey in the privacy of your home, picking and playing songs to represent each significant relationship in your past. Think about each of these relationships for the duration of the song. Were you ever motivated to try to buy or steal their love? Are you continuing this behavior? If you make passes at your friend's lovers, as Angelica did, look into that with suspicion. Our culture teaches that beautiful and expensive possessions and physical beauty will bring you love. Both will bring you lots of attention and the illusion of love. "Love" that is obtained or solicited by theft, manipulation, or seduction is on very shaky ground.

Helping Question 6.4:

How Did Your Relationship With Peers Affect Your Feelings Of Belonging?

The first group outside their family that most people relate to is a peer group. It could consist of you and one friend. More commonly peer groups, like families, consist of more than two people, who usually live in the same neighborhood. Such a club or gang, besides being rewarding in and of itself, can be a big help in compensating for, and even overcoming, early emotional deficits. The support of peers is a vital factor in giving adolescents the strength to oppose parents if necessary (and it's almost always necessary) in order to establish their own identities. If early experiences have made peer relationships difficult, as with Angelica, the difficulty of developing one's independence increases. I have had a number of clients, who, as a result of their childhood family experiences, would have landed in a mental hospital if not for one good friend or one good peer group.

I often work with people who experienced too little emotional support in their childhood and feel hopeless about achieving it in their adult lives. I always ask such clients to tell me about their closest friend during childhood. Recalling this relationship usually helps them to realize that it is possible to achieve friendship, and encourages them to search for the reasons they lack such support in their present lives.

Anthony

Anthony had no positive feelings about school until he entered junior high. There, for the first time, his need for support and encouragement was partially gratified by friendly relationships with most of his teachers. For the first time he felt accepted, even valued. With the novel feeling of security brought on by these new relationships with teachers, he became able to relate to peers more freely. He even joined the school's baseball team.

In high school Anthony vied academically and in sports with one of his classmates. After High School, they went to different colleges and after college lived in different parts of the country, but a friendship grew through correspondence and occasional visits. Later in their lives they found themselves in the same city, which let them achieve a truly intimate friendship. That achievement led Anthony to other relationships of equality, sharing, and intimacy.

Angelica

Angelica was born into a Jewish family in an all-Jewish neighborhood. Though shy, she had one good friend. She lost that friend just before she reached puberty, because her family moved to another town. There her new peers were anti-Semitic. They refused to have anything to do with her. She assumed, as most children do under such circumstances, that there must be something wrong with her if classmates and neighbors rejected her.

Angelica had forgotten all but the name of the friend she lost as a young child. Stimulated by thoughts of how her relationships with peers affected the feelings of belonging, she recalled all the happy details of that relationship. This helped her realize that her rejection in the new neighborhood she moved to as a child was a reflection of their problem, not hers.

Exercise 6.4

Review your self-narrative up to this point. Look for three "winces:" three names that make you wince. What went wrong? Try to identify factors that have caused you to withdraw from those three people, be overly aggressive, or relate in some other self-destructive way. Maybe, like Angelica, you are trying to fit into a group that will never accept you—best to give up and find one that will. Perhaps, like Anthony, you lack social skills—best to find a setting in which you can learn and practice whatever social skills you lack. Maybe, like Marie, you suffered from an emotional trauma when you were growing up resulting in exaggerated conscious and/or unconscious fears. One or more of these factors may inhibit you from relating to others in a constructive way. Get to the roots of whatever interpersonal difficulties you have and it will free you to learn how to relate to others in a more constructive manner.

Extra Mile 6.4:

If you suffered from less than optimal loving as a child (and who hasn't?) it will help you to recall when, how, and why; as it helped Angelica and Anthony.

- How many close friends do you have? If you have none, how could you develop at least one close friendship? Try joining a special interest group of some kind. Joining a men's or women's support group does it for many. If you have fewer friends than you would like, consider the axiom "If you want a friend, be a friend."

- What are the characteristics you want in a friend? Try to eliminate those you decide are unreasonable (like wanting someone to always agree with you).

- Ask someone you trust to help you learn what you need to know. Perhaps, like Marie, you were grievously wounded in the past. Make a plan for overcoming any handicap developed as a result of such a wound.

Helping Question 6.5:

Who Stuck With Who In Your Family of Origin? Who Did You Trust? Who Did You Distrust?

Marie

Marie's family of origin was emotionally more a collection of individuals than a family. At age eight, her mother remarried and she and her brother, Adam, entered the first group that, though it had serious problems, could still be called a family. It consisted of Marie and Adam, their mother, and their stepfather Leonard. In addition to Marie being seduced by Leonard, as described in her responses to CENTRAL QUESTION ONE, *WHERE DID YOU COME FROM?*, there was another problem. There were two subgroups in her new family. (1) her mother and Adam, and (2) her and Leonard.

Adam considered Leonard an enemy until after he was forty years old. By that time he had learned more about himself, and with some mellowing on the part of Leonard, their relationship improved.

As though Marie and her family didn't have enough problems, Marie's brother Adam suffered from epilepsy. Adam's seizures began shortly after Marie, at age nine, doused him with a stream of water from a garden hose. He backed up, tripped on a curb, hit his head on the sidewalk, and passed out for a few minutes. Marie believed that this brought on his seizures.

This belief strongly influenced Marie's decision to enter the nursing profession. As an RN, she became important in sharing the family's efforts to be helpful to Adam. The subgroups (1) mother-Adam and (2) Leonard-Marie, disappeared, but not their effects. It took considerable work for Marie to become aware of the childhood origins of her feelings of not belonging, except in a professional capacity, and further work before she fully overcame their effects on her life as an adult.

On the next page are the diagrams made by Marie, and her mother, covering the first seventeen years of Marie's life:

QUESTIONS TO GROW BY   107

Diagrams Made By Marie

Marie, Age 0-5:

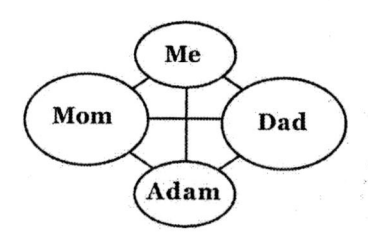

Me — Mom, Dad, Adam (connected)

Marie, Age 5-8:

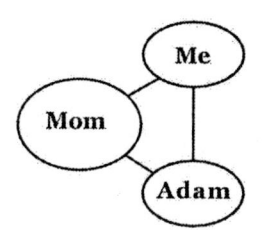

Me — Mom, Adam

Marie, Age 8-9:

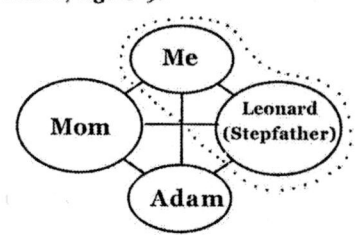

Me — Mom, Leonard (Stepfather), Adam (Me, Leonard, and Adam circled together)

Marie, Age 9-17:

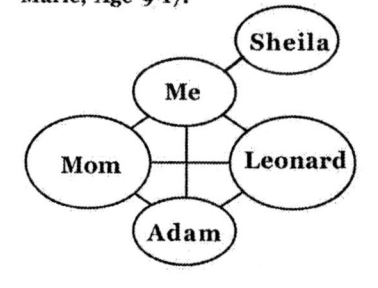

Me — Sheila, Mom, Leonard, Adam

Diagrams Made By Marie's Mother

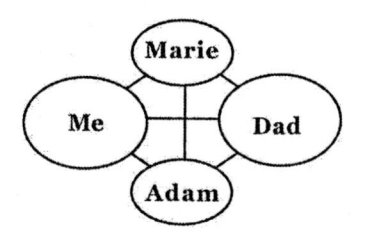

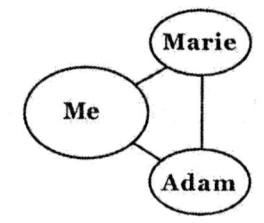

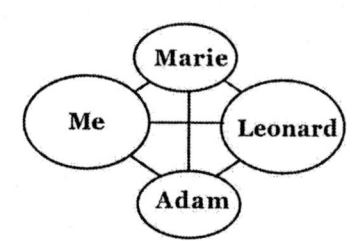

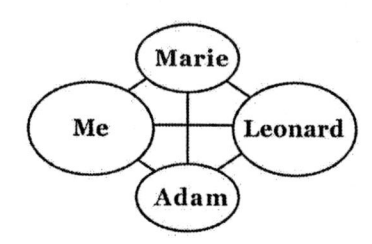

Me — Marie, Dad, Adam

Me — Marie, Adam

Me — Marie, Leonard, Adam

Me — Marie, Leonard, Adam

After she moved to a San Diego suburb at age fourteen, Marie felt especially close to her next door neighbor, Sheila. In short order, they considered themselves to be each other's best friend. Because she had been sexually molested by her stepfather at age eight, Marie became especially self-conscious as she approached adolescence and felt the powerful stirrings of sexuality. She had little confidence around boys, and became quiet and withdrawn in their presence.

Marie remembers playing a game in Junior High. The game consisted of a small group of mixed gender classmates sharing their reactions to each other. Some of the boys told Marie that it was hard to get to know her—she was standoffish. She was crushed. Sheila immediately came to her defense; refuting the description and encouraging the boys to try harder. Later she and Sheila discussed their shared feelings of shyness around boys. This, in itself, didn't solve Marie's or Sheila's problem. It was, however, a stepping stone for both of them in their shared, continuing, and ultimately successful efforts.

Fortunately, Marie and her mother discussed the relationships within their family in considerable detail. Following the directions for doing Exercise 6.5, they diagrammed the family relationships as they experienced them. As you can see from their diagrams, Marie and her mother's perceptions of the family dynamics were similar until Leonard became part of the family when Marie was eight. After showing these diagrams to each other, Marie and her mother were stimulated to discuss both the agreements and disagreements in their perceptions, which resulted in a better understanding of themselves and each other. They then talked together with Leonard. He never agreed that he had sexually molested Marie (basing his denial on the Clinton Defense; that he never actually penetrated her), but he obviously felt very guilty and apologized profusely for what he did. He claimed it was a one time thing which he stopped because of his shame and guilt. His marriage with Marie's mother was restrained for a while, but recovered, as did his relationship with Marie.

Exercise 6.5

Using the diagram made by Marie and her mother as a model, make a rough diagram of your family. Put the name of each family member in a circle the size of which indicates their importance to you. join all the circles (people) by lines. Use heavy lines to indicate especially strong connections. Draw dotted circles around subgroups. If there were significant changes in structure at particular times because of particular events, draw separate before and after diagrams. Study your diagram and use it to reconstruct the unique history of your family. Write out what you have learned by doing so.

Extra Mile 6.5:

Ask some of your friends, especially those of the opposite gender, if, in their opinion, you are unconsciously playing any roles that reflect family or sexual problems.

Helping Question 6.6:

What is the Nature Of Your Involvement in Social Groups?

Ken

When I first felt fully accepted by a social group I had no idea why it happened. It was a summer evening in Chicago. Some residents of the tenement house in which I lived were chatting on the front stoop. My friend Jim, also a resident of the tenement, and I, joined them. I was eight years old. Chicago weather is seldom balmy, but on that night it was exactly what I imagined the weather was like on a South Sea Island: a warm and lazy day became a languid and meditative evening. The usual sounds of the city were hushed, its pace slowed.

The informal group on the front stoop included senior citizens, parents, teenagers, and my friend Jim and I. We all talked easily and freely. I don't remember what we talked about, but I remember the atmosphere. Everyone's opinion was respected. No one tried to outshine anyone else. No one tried to be the center of attention. No distinction was made between adults and children, boys and girls, men and women. For one magical evening it was as though we were all members of one happy family. An evening that just happened. To my knowledge it had never happened before, and never happened again.

Not until ten years later, as a senior in high school, did I have a similar experience. Ten fellow students and I became very close during our senior year. We helped each other study, conducted mock examinations, and shared an active social life. Remembering my experience on the Chicago stoop, this time I asked my fellow students if they shared my warm feelings about the group we had created. Most of them did. But I still didn't know why this came about.

The helping questions of this chapter proved to be the key that unlocked the reasons for my positive group experience as a child on the stoop of a Chicago Tenement and as an adolescent in high school. It was a combination of my openness and the openness of these two groups. I learned to look for groups like these rather than to try to become involved with groups regardless of my estimate as to how open they were. Since then my positive group experiences have recurred with increasing frequency.

Angelica

"In my early adulthood I was so insecure that I joined any group that would have me, while repressing any negative feelings I had about the group. After going through QUESTIONS, I realized that not allowing feelings to come into consciousness doesn't eliminate them. In retrospect, I concluded that my repressed feelings were expressed by my sometimes sarcastic and condescending tone of voice. Through self-evaluation, and acting on its results, I am now more self-aware, which has led to facing and expressing negative feelings directly rather than indirectly. If this doesn't work I consider leaving such a group."

Exercise 6.6:

Practically everyone has suffered from rejection by a group at some time in their lives. Identify a time when this happened to you. What did that group have that you wanted? Picture them now, as realistically as you can, perhaps at a reunion. Do these people still hold the allure they had when you first were in contact with them? What do you want to ask and/or tell them?

Extra Mile 6.6:

Angelica's pilgrimage through different groups helped her find what she was looking for in groups. First she defined what she was looking for, then helped create it. Keep her story in mind if you are looking for a group to belong to or would like to improve the interpersonal relationships of a group in which you already belong. Look for the key elements that work for you in a group. These elements can help you strengthen groups with family-like potential, as well as avoid those that do not show such potential.

- What are you looking for?
- What are you doing to bring it about?

Helping Question 6.7:

What is the Nature and Quality of Your Involvement In Work Groups?

In the last twenty five years there has been a dramatic increase in social and family life research. One of its most important findings is that all of us, unless we learn to behave differently, repeat in business and other groups the behavior we originally learned in the families we were born and brought up in.

Here are some examples from my experiences working with a management consulting firm in New York City:

- A board meeting where the Chair has just made a decision that threatens and alienates some of the very people who will have to carry it out. Although there is a tremendous amount of resentment and tension, it is suppressed. It's Stiff-Upper-Lip-Time. No one speaks up, shows anger, or ventures a dissenting opinion. Instead, everyone looks calm and smiles confidently, while the possibility that they may be fired or want to quit is being considered by one or more company executives.

- A company that has to choose between two programs because two managers are jockeying for winning positions. Instead of pooling their ideas and coming up with one superior plan, all their energy is focused in a tug-of-war over whose ideas are "right."

- Five bright workers are expending great effort to make sure they "look good" and that nobody "gets" anything on them. Effort that should be used to increase production is used to amass great numbers of Cover-Your-Ass Memos.

The above are examples of workers unconsciously playing out roles they learned in their families of origin. Not until they came to know themselves better was any constructive change in their interaction possible.

Anthony

In Anthony's family of origin his grandfather was the controlling influence. Later in his life, as described in his responses to CENTRAL QUESTION ONE, WHERE DID YOU COME FROM?, Anthony left his family because of disenchantment with his grandfather's illegal business. When he was growing up he was not aware of this, and modeled himself after his grandfather's commanding, authoritative way of life.

After Anthony left home he established a law office which eventually employed a series of young attorneys. The reason it was "a series" was because Anthony treated young attorneys in the same authoritarian way that his grandfather had treated him. The result was a rapid turnover of young attorneys until he acquired some insight into his part in causing it.

Angelica

Because of her ambivalent relationship with her authoritarian father, Angelica alternated between being authoritative and submissive with men. This got her into considerable difficulty. Sometimes she was overbearing and sometimes too submissive. As she gained insight into the unconscious factors behind her ambivalence, she has gradually thought through the role she thinks is appropriate rather than being at the mercy of her past. This has markedly reduced her ambivalence in her personal as well as her business relations with men.

"From Innocence to Insight" was the summarizing title Angelica gave to her responses to CENTRAL QUESTION SIX, *WHO ARE YOU?* Through her responses she became aware of the considerable handicaps of her early years (an over-stern father; a preoccupied mother; being rejected by her classmates and neighbors). She first learned to understand her early self-defeating attempts to overcome these handicaps, then learned some better ways of doing so. To this day she continues to keep track of her progress. She will continue to grow emotionally for the rest of her life.

Exercise 6.7:

Trace the influence of parental models on your behavior in your work-world. How do these influences inform the way you treat those above and those below you? The examples of Anthony, Angelica, Marie, and me will hopefully inspire you to become aware of the factors that most influence your behavior even if the specific influences you were exposed to were very different from those we were exposed to.

Extra Mile 6.7:

Ask the people in your current work group how they perceive your behavior, with special emphasis on anything that they think interferes with the group's effectiveness. Construct and institute a new program that includes changes based on what the people in your current work group have said. Ask them for another evaluation after six months.

The preceding helping questions (6.1 through 6.7) were designed to help you understand how your history of belonging has influenced your present feelings of belonging. The following final helping question relevant to CENTRAL QUESTION SIX, *WHO ARE YOU?* is designed to help you complete your understanding of your present, in conjunction with an understanding of your past, to aim for a future that will be better than either.

Helping Question 6.8:

How Are You Doing In Your Present Family? Are There Changes You Want To Make?

A young man who was waited on hand and foot as a child and adolescent can't understand why his wife finds it inconsiderate that he never picks up after himself. He says he's too busy supporting the family to be involved in such trivialities.

A young woman who was sexually abused by her father has sex with any man who wants it without a thought about whether she wants it. She regards herself as a free spirit.

A mother who competed desperately with a younger sister rarely complements her daughter. She says she doesn't want to give her a swelled head.

We know that what we learn in childhood is central to how we behave as adults. Without insight, often the only difference between the two is that childish behavior in adults is usually covered by a veneer of logical-sounding face-saving rationalizations.

Exercise 6.8:

Write down an aspect of yourself that at least two people have complained about or that bothers you. Create a vignette about it like one of those cited immediately after Helping Question 6.5. Make yourself the central character and express your problem, the childhood reason or reasons that encouraged it, followed by the rationalization that you use to continue it.

Extra Mile 6.8:

Share the vignette you created in response to Exercise 3.6 with one or both of the person(s) who made the complaint. Then:

- Practice behaving in a way that will eliminate the complaint.
- After three months check with the person or persons you shared your vignette with. If one or both doesn't see any change, check again after further effort. Keep doing this until you get a positive response.

After exploring CENTRAL QUESTION SIX: *WHO ARE YOU?* we turn to PART FOUR, YOUR FUTURE: THE WORLD'S FUTURE, followed by CENTRAL QUESTION SEVEN, *WHO DO YOU WANT TO BECOME?*

PART IV

Your Future: The World's Future

○ ○
The good of the whole begins with the individual.

—*Sandra Marshall*

This book has discussed and demonstrated the intimate connection between the stories we tell ourselves (Self-Narratives) and the lives we lead, with special attention to the way some self-narratives can halt emotional growth in some areas of life. It encourages you to become fully aware of your story, and then to check it against your values and what you have learned in the course of your life. This may lead to a revision of your story, which can result in a revision of your life. I believe that self-knowledge is essential to achieving a happy fulfilled life, and that individuals who achieve such a life are much more likely to contribute positively to their families, communities, nations, and the world.

CENTRAL QUESTION SEVEN

WHO DO YOU WANT TO BECOME?

○ ○

I'll tell you something
I think you'll understand,
Then I'll say something,
I want to hold your hand

—John Lennon &
Paul McCartney

Your response to CENTRAL QUESTION SEVEN, *WHO DO YOU WANT TO BECOME?* will summarize a combination of (1) your current emotional posture toward yourself and the world and (2) your current self-aspirations. Since these factors are most strongly influenced by your emotional history I encourage you to study your Self-Narrative as a means of reconsidering your life in the light of these two factors. Doing so is likely to change at least some of your current feelings. You've seen some examples of how it did so for others. To help you with your self-searching, Angelica, Anthony, Marie, and I will share our Self-Narratives. As part of going through QUESTIONS we each made up titles summarizing responses to the questions and exercises of each chapter as well as a title summarizing the overall changes we have made in ourselves. In what follows I introduce the Self-Narrative of each one of us and the distinctive title each one of us has given to our particular Self-Narrative.

The questions and exercises of preceding chapters encouraged you to compose a diary-like presentation of your life. This chapter encourages you to complete the story of your life (Self Narrative), based upon the most significant happenings of your life and their meaning for you. I think that you will find that your Self Narrative will develop a life of its own as you go from Chapter to Chapter, with Who Do You Want To Become? as its final focus. The responses of Angelica, Anthony, and Marie, that are reported on the following pages were written by them. I have added some opening and closing comments to their accounts. The opening quote from Lennon and McCartney is meant to convey our wish that you regard us as your companions on this journey, which we now joyfully, hand in hand, complete.

Helping Question 7.1

Do Your Images of Your Future Reveal a Direction and Goal Which Encourages Continuing Growth?

Angelica: From Automaton to Liberated Woman

Becoming aware of unconscious fears requires an exploration of defenses. Weakening of defenses facilitates coming in contact with your true self. Unless it is directed by your true self, "growth" may consist of a strengthening of defenses.

An awareness of fears can stimulate growth. As she responded to QUESTIONS, Angelica tried to be sensitive to any hint of fear that came up for her. She tried to spell out her fears as clearly as possible:

"Why were my fears buried so deeply? I think because they were so elemental and forceful that I was afraid I would be immobilized by them. One is my fear of physical harm. When I look back on my childhood I remember being spanked by my father but don't remember the fear, anger or shame. I am afraid of physical attack by men. Some of that I attribute to world violence, but I've come to realize that most of it comes from more personal sources. I have had feelings of panic when staying alone. A window would rattle, a door would creak, and I would begin sweating, heart pounding, alert for an attack.

"I have a greater fear that is harder to describe and more difficult to examine: The fear of having no control over life events such as accidents, floods and random shootings. This fear extends to everyone I love, for I know I can't protect them. They can be taken from me at any moment, without warning. Since going through QUESTIONS I find myself more and more frequently breaking through my wall of fear and allowing myself to feel the cauldron of pain and suffering that is bubbling inside of me. I have been surprised that feeling the pain, coupled with the knowledge that the pain will pass, has begun to free me from it.

"Meditation has helped. Getting in touch with my physical body gives me clues. Tight breathing or aching muscles are signposts. Tears are another signpost. Recognizing that I've outgrown some fears is useful in approaching new ones. For example, I had a fear of speaking in public for many years. I think this came from my childhood equation: not doing what your expected to do equals being naughty, which equals loss of love. Whenever I stood in front of a group, I felt my heart pounding. To me the audience looked critical and bored even before I started. That has changed. I now feel more at ease and my audiences have lost most of their ability to frighten me. What happened? On an intellectual level I realize my former level of fear was unfounded. Instead of ignoring it, which was my first approach to trying to overcome it, I began working with it in a deliberate way.

"Feeling the fear and living with it taught me that it was not going to overwhelm me. Experiencing it directly has helped to dissipate it. I now keep it in my awareness and live with it as a friend rather than an enemy.

"'Becoming' is part of everyone's life. What has changed for me in the recent past is that becoming more self-aware has become more and more important to me as I came to realize how important it is if one is to become fully human."

Angelica joined the National Organization of Women (NOW) and began to attend a woman's support group. When she shared some of what she learned in NOW, her husband was very troubled. He was even more troubled the following year when the baby arrived and Angelica tried to get him to take part of the responsibility for the baby's care. "That's a woman's job!" he declared. The battle was on; and it didn't stop until they were divorced four years later.

These developments resulted in a redefining of her priorities: physical beauty became less important and emotional maturity went to the top of the list. Her life began more and more to reflect this change in priorities. People who knew her before these changes would certainly experience her differently today.

Angelica found that in addition to her work on QUESTIONS, contacts with spiritually advanced people, was also a help. Here is her description of one of those experiences:

"I have have met a few people who I consider to be highly developed spiritually. I have found them generally to be highly developed emotionally as well. These contacts, some of them very brief, have been very important to me. When I finished my M.A., I was a candidate for a teaching and research appointment. I was interviewed by the President of the University, and the President, Dean, and Comptroller of the College of Education. To my surprise, the person who made the deepest impression on me during this round of interviews was the Comptroller. He radiated peacefulness and a dedication to the health and happiness of others. A financial expert altruistically dedicated to education, a combination I had never met before."

The sequence of Angelica's dreams reveals some of the important changes that have taken place in her emotional life from childhood to the present. She discusses them in her self narrative as follows:

"The first dream I remember was a recurring one, from when I was eight years old and had just started school in my new home with my mother and her new husband. I dreamt I was swimming between two huge groups of pilings in the docking space of the Hudson River Ferry. The water was dirty and slimy. A ferry was entering the docking space. I was caught between the incoming ferry and the shore, underneath the drawbridge over which cars passed from the ferry to the shore. This dream recurred at irregular intervals for over a year. In retrospect, I realize that it represented my feelings about my life at that time. I felt caught in a dangerous place between my mother and stepfather (the groupings of pilings in my dream). Difficulties in school made the problem worse. When my tensions about school relaxed, the dream recurred less frequently. Then I developed my mechanical woman fantasy and the dream ceased. Needless to say, the essential problem was not solved but only hidden. I found it necessary to go over and over this period of my life because the mechanical woman fantasy, though it was useful during my childhood, interfered with my adult life. As a result of exercising this emotional protection, I didn't develop the emotional maturity necessary for intimate relationships, and was overwhelmed by the loving and romantic feelings that broke through in my last year of college.

"A dream I've had from time to time in the last year is that I am flying into orbit around the earth. The feeling is both scary and exhilarating: going into the unknown, leaving all previous supports behind. I regard it as a positive dream, in line with the positive though scary at-the-time changes I have made in my life."

Exercise 7.1:

Angelica's Self-Narrative clearly reveals her progress in a direction of goals that are realistic and encourage further growth. Does your Self-Narrative reflect the same progress? Or does it imply a closing down, a retreat from possibilities for further growth? If it does the latter, please reconsider in the light of your self-narrative.

Helping Question 7.2:

If Much of Your Growth Has been Accidental or Situational, How Can You Position Yourself to Grow Intentionally?

Anthony: From Self-Righteous to Self-Affirming

"My parents and grandparents were unquestionably the strongest influences on the development of my personality. When I was growing up I especially felt the influence of my father and grandfather. They were in many ways opposites: my grandfather was impulsive, self-centered, a heavy drinker; my father was frugal, self-denying, and over-controlled. They left me with these opposites and a struggle to find and stay within the golden mean of each. An example of where I succeeded is my resolution of my problem with alcohol. An example of where I still have work to do is staying within the law while driving an automobile: I have never had a serious accident, but I get an average of at least one traffic ticket per year.

"I saw my grandfather as weak and ineffectual. I didn't realize I loved him until after he died. I struggled for years with hostile feelings toward my father. I didn't realize I loved him until I finally ended twenty years of practically no contact."

The stages of growth in infancy are not always completed in infancy. If not, they may be completed later in life with one's parents or parent substitutes. If they are not completed in childhood or thereafter, full psychological birth (to borrow the term used by Margaret Mahler) does not occur. The first stage of human emotional growth is characterized by complete dependence on a caregiver. The second stage is characterized by the need to experiment with separation from the caregiver for limited periods of time. In the third stage psychological birth has occurred: the growing infant has succeeded in becoming a separate person who is beginning to choose who and to what extent he/she will be involved with others.

Anthony's struggles with fully achieving psychological birth are not yet complete. His marriage has elements of struggle over his wish that he and Angelica should be one, while she wants more differentiation. Neither of them has fully completed psychological birth. Though Angelica says she wants to be more separate, this wish is, in part, a rebellion against her dependence on Anthony.

An important reason we pick the people we marry is that, to varying degrees, most of us feel, consciously or unconsciously, that there is something missing in our lives that the other person can supply. There is almost always truth in this belief. When each supplies the other with what they need, the result is usually a happy marriage. Unfortunately, this doesn't always happen, especially if the couple can't or doesn't acknowledge the growth potential of differences. I have known many couples who separated because of the very differences that originally brought them together. Here's how Anthony expressed this:

"It was a chastening experience for me to realize that among the important reasons I married Angelica was that, in part, I wanted to be taken care of the way a mother takes care of her child. I later found that one of the important reasons she married me was that, in part, she wanted to be taken care of the way a father takes care of his child. That realization and helped us to help each other work on our individual developmental problems. We are determined to succeed so that we relate to each other in a more mature and satisfying way.

"The biggest immediate benefit I got from going through QUESTIONS was the realization that cutting myself off from my family in my early twenties was a self-defeating way of trying to solve my problem with them. Armed with this insight, I reestablished a connection with them. This resulted in my developing a broader view of what it means to have mature human relations—to understand and forgive. This has helped me not only in my relationships with family members, but with all my human relationships.

"Going through QUESTIONS resulted in an extensive review of the central values of my life. The following list, in order of priority, is the result:

- The quality of my human relationships.
- Being a creative and productive person.
- Living in an orderly and aesthetically pleasing environment
- Helping make the world a better place to live in.

"My number-one value, quality of my human relationships, means to me a stronger commitment to love, democracy, and freedom, since I believe they are vital to good human relationships. This, of course, has involved abandonment of the chauvinistic view of the relationship between men and women that I was brought up to believe in. It also involves developing the ability to downgrade relationships that are unsatisfactory and unlikely to improve and to upgrade those that are more promising. The improvement I seek is primarily developing greater openness, sincerity, understanding, and depth.

"My second most important value, being a creative and productive person, was not on the first or second draft of my list. It wasn't until the third draft that I realized I had left something out. My feeling about myself, which strongly affects my relationships with others, varies with my feelings about my overall level of creativity and productivity. That is not to say that I have to produce a breakthrough in human creativity or productivity to feel okay. Something as simple as fixing the vacuum cleaner or learning anything useful or enlightening is enough to sustain me from day to day.

"Value number three, living in an orderly and aesthetically pleasing environment, was also left out of my original list. In its place I had "money." Though necessary for an orderly and aesthetically pleasing environment, money did not properly describe the value I had in mind. I no longer feel the need to earn large amounts of money. I am no longer a slave to the American culture's dedication to the idea that the road to happiness is to become rich and famous. I do want to earn enough to maintain my present somewhat above average standard of living.

"I regret that I cannot put value number four, my most altruistic value, anywhere but at the bottom of the list. If I come to more fully live my philosophy of life perhaps my life will become so satisfactory that I will be able to give this value a higher priority."

Before his encounter with QUESTIONS Anthony believed that his emotions were appropriate; after it he acknowledged that there were areas where they were not. He also realized that it was in his best interests to identify the fears and/or ignorance causing areas of immaturity to persist. These two realizations have helped him make continuing progress in reducing fear and ignorance, resulting in continuing growth in emotional maturity.

Exercise 7.2:

Anthony's Self Narrative shows how growth can occur as a result of accidental and/or situational factors. He, however, had stopped conscious self-directed growth until he got himself into a Questions Group. It wasn't easy for him to reveal himself in that group or any other group, but as a result of doing so, he is now able to do it on his own in the various groups he is now a member of. Are you able to reveal the things that disturb you in any of the groups that you are a member of? If not, decide what is the best approach to doing so in the group you feel is most likely to welcome it, and do it!

Extra Mile

Like Anthony, and Angelica, make your own "hero trail." List three of your current heroes. What do they share? Specify the changes you want to make to better emulate them. How will you make them? Follow this by systematic practice until you "feel in your bones" that you have succeeded.

Helping Question 7.3:

Have You Focused On a Particular Aspect of Human Culture and Ignored Others, Such as the Arts, Philosophy, or Spirituality?

Marie: Up From Slavery

"During my childhood I felt like an orphan, which is essentially what I was. Throughout my childhood, adolescence, and young adulthood, I was unconsciously looking for a parental figure I could attach myself to. My relationship with my mother, bad as it was, played a central role in the development of my personality. As a young woman I found myself acting like her. The worst of that was reflected in my relationships with men. Being seduced by my stepfather at an early age made this problem much worse. Examining my formative years has helped me develop a better relationship with myself and my husband. I feel hopeful about my future."

I asked Marie what she believed was the most significant thing she learned from her Self-Narrative. She replied that she had learned a way of approaching emotional problems which continued to help her. When I asked her for an example she asked me if I remembered her "twenty year obsession." I remembered it well. It was her first serious love affair. It lasted four months, during which she was so infatuated that she forgot almost everything else, including her personal freedom. When Bert told her he no longer loved her, she was devastated. For a year she thought of him several times a day, every day. After several years the frequency of thoughts about him gradually decreased, but continued to occur at least once a day. She went on to tell me:

"After I completed my self-narrative, I still had obsessive thoughts about Bert, even though I felt very good about my relationship with my husband. I had pretty much resigned myself to having obsessive thoughts about Bert for the rest of my life. Last year, after an early morning hike through the woods surrounding a Sierra Club cabin in the mountains east of San Diego, it occurred to me that I hadn't thought about Bert for over a week! I had finally put a significant distance between myself and those futile, obsessive thoughts!
"I sat down and wrote a poem which helped me to further free myself. I rewrote it several times before it took its present form:

> Here I Sit
>
> writing words you will never read
> or ever know were written.
>
> A five mile hike
> and a twenty year odyssey
> have brought me to this place.
>
> To the realization that
> I'm through with you at last

> Through with you
> because I'm through with
> part of myself.
> The part that thought I'd die
> if I wasn't loved by my father.
>
> I wasn't loved by him
> and I'm not loved by you.
> But I am loved by myself.
>
> It's enough.
> I survive and prosper.

Trying to find a father or a mother in a lover is not unusual. In our culture it's part of falling in love for everyone but the most unusually mature. Like any emotional problem, it can't be solved until the person who has it precisely defines what the real problem is. In the course of tracing her emotional history Marie discovered its real source, after which the solution came almost automatically.

As she put it:
"I got practically no fathering as I grew up. The promise of fathering from my stepfather turned out to be abuse, so I repressed my need. Repression only drove it underground, where it gained strength. I wasn't aware of this, so I had no way of understanding it. When I became aware of it through writing my Self-Narrative, I could deal with it. I came to realize, to feel in my bones, that, at my age, I don't need the fathering I needed when I was growing up. I am free at last!!"

When we are infants, the only source of love for most of us in our culture is our mother and father or other caregiver(s). We have to get it from at least one of them or we don't get it at all. When you are an infant, not getting love from either mother or father could literally result in your death. We have no choice but to seek it from them, no matter how pitiably meager the supply. That was reality for Marie as an infant, as it is for all of us. It isn't reality for her as a grown person, as it isn't for the rest of us, but it took finding a way to define the real problem for her to take this in.

Marie is still somewhat prone to obsessive thoughts, but they have no chance of lasting twenty years! Now, as soon as she notices that she is obsessing, she searches for the fear or insecurity behind it. Working through such fears and insecurities sooner or later ends the obsession with the gift of emotional and spiritual growth. She has come to the point where she now welcomes becoming aware of fears and insecurities because facing them enables her to solve them, and solving them increases her energy, her appreciation of self, others, and the world at large.

I first mentioned Marie in the Introduction to this book with the statement, "Marie couldn't enjoy sex." The hope of overcoming this problem motivated her to undertake QUESTIONS. In the process she was able to define her fears, one of which, her fear of sex, had developed into near-paralysis of her sexual responsiveness. Her sexual near-paralysis was really part of her near-paralysis in life in general. She has loosened up in many areas, both professionally and personally. Her progress in both areas are testified to by her recently enrolling in a graduate nursing program leading to a certificate as a nurse-practitioner, and her new-found passion for, appreciation of, and talent in, writing poetry.

Over time fears and ignorance can diminish without insight, as in the example of Marie's twenty year obsession, but are rarely completely resolved. Insight is much quicker and more effective.

Exercise 7.3:

Marie's current Self—Narrative reflects how the solution of her emotional problems around love and sex inhibited her emotional growth and how she was able to overcome her inhibition with the help of a new source of strength: poetry. Do you have an inhibition that wasn't overcome in the process of going through QUESTIONS? If so, entering into one or more aspects of human culture you may have ignored may be the path to your salvation.

Helping Question 7.4:

Are There Specific Steps You Can Take To Promote Further Growth in Yourself?

Ken: From Emotional Detachment to Enduring Love

The most important thing that happened to me as a result of responding to QUESTIONS was a shift in my values. From the American eastern seaboard culture where I was brought up, plus my mother's need for status, I absorbed an unbridled ambition. This was first checked by coming face to face with the realities of what I could expect to accomplish, and then, more definitively, by a change in my values. Now my ambition is more focused on wanting to fulfill my values rather than the values of my culture.

From my upbringing I absorbed the standard ideas of what it meant to be male, many of which I have reassessed as chauvinistic and self-defeating. From later reflections on my life and on life in general, I absorbed a passion for democracy which, for me, has grown from a slogan to a central value. It guides me in many ways, including my efforts to find a more enlightened concept of what it means to be a male.

My first marriage failed in spite of my efforts to preserve it, and I didn't know why. What's more, I didn't think I was going to find the whys of this failure if I stayed in the routine of my life. Even vacations had become part of that routine.

I decided to take off a year and see if that led to any significant change. I called it my 'sabbatical.' It started with what I hoped would be a round-the-world cruise with a friend who owned a forty foot motor-sailer. To our dismay, we found we couldn't stand each other by the time we got to St. Thomas, U. S. Virgin Islands. I rented a room in St. Thomas, bought and outfitted a 29 foot trimaran sloop, and recruited a crew of two who agreed to help me sail it around the world. After spending three months outfitting the boat, we set sail in May of 1985. In the middle of the afternoon of our fourth day out the boat sprang a leak which filled its cabin with water. At about ten o'clock that night we sent an S.O.S., by flashlight, to a passing freighter. It bore down on us, sheared off one of the two pontoons that were keeping us afloat, then made a U-turn, and came alongside of what was left of our boat. They lowered a heavy net off the side of the freighter, with the help of which we left our boat, the decks of which were by this time awash, and climbed aboard the freighter.

After these two ill-fated attempts, I thought perhaps I should try another way to go around the world. I bought a round-the-world airline ticket and spent six months roughly following the equator from New York around the world and back to New York. In the course of that trip I stayed for varying periods in nineteen countries. My emotional and spiritual growth received a great forward impetus when I spent two months in India. I traveled up and down the country visiting various gurus, spending ten days at a Meditation Center and ten days at an Ashram. Gradually, these experiences led me to the conviction that emotional growth was a necessary preliminary before I could hope to achieve spiritual growth. I got completely out of the routine of my life, which helped me get a better perspective on it. I also met many people with different lifestyles. I came back a changed person.

When I returned to the USA, at the age of sixty three, I had nowhere to live. My mother was living alone in a two bedroom house in New Jersey, so I moved in with her. I re-experienced many of the feelings I had experienced with her when I was growing up, only this time I had whatever maturity I had gained in the course of sixty three years. By the time I moved out, to start a new life in California, I had not only increased insight into my earlier relationships, but some actual experience in establishing and practicing new and better relationships. I also had some important insights into my contribution to the breakup of my first marriage, the most important of which is summarized in the title of this summary of my Self-Narrative.

In California I established a part-time psychotherapy practice and started working on QUESTIONS. After ten years of working on it I produced a manuscript which I shared with my clients and used as a basis for teaching a course in human relations at the First Unitarian-Universalist Church of San Diego. My own personal work on QUESTIONS and feedback from clients, members of the UU Church, friends, writing teachers, colleagues and editors resulted in the book you are reading. At age eighty three, I regard it as my legacy to my children and anyone else who finds it of interest.

Learning more about myself has been important to me ever since I took a course in human relations at M.I.T. as an undergraduate biology major. With the help of a hypnosis demonstration our instructor not only told us, but demonstrated, that most human behavior is guided by unconscious rather than conscious motives. World War II, my experience with developing and practicing QUESTIONS, and the advent of 9/11, are representative of experiences that have intensified my learning about how people and societies function and malfunction and motivated me to present my ideas in this regard to anyone who is willing to listen and give me some feedback.

Which brings me to an important advantage of being eighty three years old. As a result of living that long, I have a large store of life experiences to review if I care to. And I care to. I find doing so very helpful. Fortunately, I have had the time and opportunity to do it. It has been an important activity of mine for the last twenty years.

In the course of these activities I have come to believe that spiritual growth is as important as biological, intellectual, and emotional growth. These three types of growth are separate from each other but interdependent. Healthy biological growth encourages healthy emotional growth just as healthy emotional growth encourages healthy spiritual growth. This book is about emotional growth, not about biological, intellectual, or spiritual growth; but I believe it is important to mention their relationships with each other. Human beings interest in different kinds of development has shifted during the time they have been on earth. Individuals interests have always differed from one individual to another at the same time that the majority of people's interests have shifted in an evolutionary manner. I have found that people who believe that they have achieved a satisfactory level of emotional maturity are more likely than the average to also be interested in spiritual development.

I have come to believe that all humans are born with a spark of divinity. I believe that nurturing and increasing that spark in ourselves and others is the most important of life's activities.

I remember my first wife phoning me from time to time during the early years of our marriage just to say "I love you.' Unhappily that practice disappeared in our later years together, but I still fondly remember it as one expression of her spark of divinity, and it nurtured my spark of divinity. I sometimes now spontaneously call my present wife just to say "I love you."

I remember my daughter Hilary at age eight. We took a walk around the neighborhood of our home. We walked about two blocks when some friends of Hilary's spotted her and came running toward us shouting "Hilary!" "Hilary!" They were so glad to see her! Hilary went off happily to play with them, each member of the group enjoying and enhancing the divinity of that group of children.

I remember my daughter Cindy when she was ten. She had bought a birthday present for her mother, and was so eager to give it to her that I had to restrain her from giving it to her a day early. That was typical of my divine Cindy: from an early age getting more pleasure from giving than receiving—an unusual trait for a girl brought up in the materialistic culture of the United States.

I remember my son Doug at age twelve. He organized and ran a pet show in our backyard. He made dozens of wooden stakes suitable for animals of all sizes and invited the neighborhood to bring their pets. At least a dozen children did so. There were prizes for the largest, the smallest, the most unusual, and the best looking. Doug loved animals of all kinds, and was in his glory, as were the other participants. He created, managed, and thoroughly enjoyed the show.

The sparks of divinity in every being who participated were enhanced, including sparks of divinity in the animals.

I count my 80th birthday, as the happiest birthday I've had so far. My dear wife and her parents were with me, as were my two daughters, their husbands and sons. When a group like that gets together, their sparks of divinity can combine and produce a palpable atmosphere of divinity. That happened at my 80th birthday party and continues to happen at an accelerated rate in various of my current life experiences.

Anyone's life can be considered along a continuum from no consciousness of self and others toward sainthood. Applying this measure to the lives of the four people we have considered in detail; none of them achieved sainthood, but all made some progress in that direction.

Exercise 7.4:

Spell out the interpersonal, spiritual, philosophical, sociological or other dimension of yourself that you would like to enhance. Take a step toward such enhancement by selecting an activity that you think would help you, such as an adult education course, an Elderhostel trip, or involving yourself in the study of another culture, and do it!

Further Reflections

Joseph Campbell spent his life studying the themes and motifs of the world's mythologies. He summarized what he learned as "The Hero's Journey", a myth that he finds in various forms in all mythologies. He describes its general outlines as, "A hero ventures forth from the world of common day into a region of supernatural wonder: fabulous forces are there encountered and a decisive victory is won. The hero comes back from this mysterious adventure with the power to bestow boons on his fellow humans."

The portions of the lives of Angelica, Anthony, Marie, and me that are narrated in this book could all be described as heroes' journeys. Giving yourself time and space for emotional growth can be made a regular part of your life. I know one couple who go away for three days twice a year to review the state of their union and plan goals for the next six months and the next five years. Other people go on religious retreats, meditation retreats, or encounter weekends. There are many opportunities available for review and reflection to help you on your journey. The important thing is to find what suits you and then do it. To quote Campbell, "Find your bliss!"

Not infrequently, in the course of thinking about the questions in this book, people change their priorities. Review what you have done in various situations and what you would do if you happened to find yourself in that same situation today. It is also useful to imagine yourself in situations you have never been in and then imagine what you would do in them. Compose your own epitaph.

Using your imagination in these ways will help you make progress in clarifying the hierarchy and consistency of your values.

A major problem many of us have is a discrepancy between thoughts and feelings. At home, in school, and in society we are taught what we are supposed to feel. Often we feel differently, but represent ourselves as feeling what we think we are supposed to feel. After years of doing this, we sometimes can no longer distinguish between what we really feel and what we think we feel. This split between thought and feeling represents an attenuation of our most precious human capacity: consciousness. It represents the opposite of what this book is about: self-awareness coming from the heart, without which there can be only superficial self-knowledge. In its extreme, this split leads to psychosis. In everyday life it isn't uncommon to meet people who, though not diagnosed as psychotic, come very close.

One woman I knew developed the habit of treating every personal problem as though it was a joke. At her husband's funeral, though he had been the center of her life for forty years, she was all laughs and smiles. This wasn't an act in the usual sense. She genuinely believed this was the proper way to deal with his death, and I'm sure that for a time at least she convinced herself that she really felt as lighthearted as she portrayed herself. This, of course, prevented her friends from fully showing their sympathy and thereby further removed her from her grief. By not allowing herself to experience grief she saved herself from facing it but may have made it unresolvable. Her suppressed grief will probably break through at some point, and when it does, it will have gained strength. It will drive her into either insight or psychosis.

The film *The Pawnbroker* illustrates this tragically self-defeating type of disconnection. A Jewish professor and his family are arrested and sent to a Nazi concentration camp. He experiences many horrors including the deaths of his wife and two children. He survives and becomes a pawnbroker in the U.S.. He successfully suppresses his concentration camp experiences at the cost of cutting himself off from any emotionally meaningful human contact, which results in further tragedies.

In addition to the hazard to ourselves, separating thoughts and feelings is also a hazard to others. It is often very difficult (and in some contexts impossible) to know what someone feels if they themselves don't know, and give out misleading signals. What such people really feel will be expressed only in situations where they are temporarily caught off guard. This was the case with the woman I spoke of earlier. Occasionally some of her real feelings would slip through, in some indirect way, but if they did she immediately covered them up. If confronted with them, she denied them.

Like many people, I generally have little trouble being aware of what I am thinking. But I do have trouble at times with knowing what I am feeling. When this happens, I find that reading through my changing story of my life is helpful. Conducting a written inner dialogue between my thoughts and feelings is also helpful, not only in becoming aware of what I'm feeling, but also in resolving conflicts between thoughts and feelings. After conducting such a dialogue I act on whatever conclusion I come to, even if I am not completely sure of it. When I do, I either find it satisfactory or else it leads to further conflict, further internal dialogue, and eventually to satisfaction. I never expect to find myself with no conflict between emotion and reason, but it is eminently worth striving for. The result of such striving is a closer approach to that ideal.

Going over the important events of their lives in the context of the changing stories of their lives has helped Anthony, Marie, Angelica, and me (as I hope it will help you) to make more sense out of where we've been and where we want to go. There is no question that our genetic and personal histories crucially affect our growth and development. However, other factors play an important part in making us who and what we are. Sometimes they overrule both our genetic and personal histories. As Anthony put it. "I don't know what all the forces that rule us are, but I have no doubt that thinking is one of them." Einstein once said the most important question a person can ask is, 'Is the universe friendly?' I believe it is. One reason I believe this is because I also believe that believing it will help it become so.

Like many people, I want to grow toward a larger underlying goal than self-interest. When I first conceived this as a goal, I believed that it can only be achieved by self-sacrifice. I found, to my great gratification, that although it involves what many regard as self-sacrifice, moving in this direction is actually more satisfying and gratifying than moving in the direction of self-interest. I and many others have discovered that in addition to the moral reasons for seeking it, the measure of happiness we achieve is directly proportional to the degree we achieve it.

Over an archway which is the entrance to the Delphic Oracle in the mountains of Greece is the inscription KNOW THYSELF. I wrote QUESTIONS to help you metaphorically walk through that arch and to help you help your family, social group, community, state, nation, and world walk through it.

Epilogue

> °
> *Unless we become the change we wish to see in the world*
> *No change will ever take place.*
>
> —Mahatma Gandhi

Thinking about these questions, which are designed to help individuals attain emotional maturity, stimulated me to think about what I regard as the most important question facing the world today: "How can nations be helped to achieve emotional maturity?"

I believe working toward emotional maturity as a nation is analogous to working toward emotional maturity as a family. Certainly if one member of a family moves in that direction she/he can influence his or her entire family to move in that direction. This was illustrated by Anthony, who first did it as an individual, and then helped his family do it. If one influential nation were to move significantly toward emotional maturity it could stimulate other nations to at least attempt it. The U.S. is in a unique position to be that nation.

There are people who say we will never eliminate war. I say, along with Barbara Hubbard, Martin Luther King Jr., and many others, that at this point in human history we can take charge of our individual and social evolution and see to it that we evolve to the point that there will be no more war. Such evolution will require that a majority of us achieve sufficient emotional maturity to inspire our nation to take a posture that may inspire other nations to do likewise. Our achievement of democracy and of sometimes treating former enemies with compassion has in the past inspired other nations. As Sandra Marshall says, as the opening words of every issue of INFORMATION PRESS, "The good of the whole begins with the individual. Let it begin with you! One person can make a difference."

A main thesis of QUESTIONS, is that a reliable way to understand ourselves and others is to explore our and their histories. The U.S. began its history by introducing and strengthening democracy within our own borders, which, in the past, inspired some nations to do likewise. It is now time to encourage greater emotional maturity in ourselves, our families, our communities, our country, and the rest of the world.

If, instead of seeking triumph over other nations, we made and lived by a Declaration of Interdependence (to borrow the terminology of Will Hutton, an English author of a book by that name) we would inspire other nations to do likewise. This would make it possible to establish a true United Nations which would be empowered to deal with international crises in an emotionally mature way, instead of, at best, the medieval way of doing things that currently seems to guide the principal nations of the world.

Bibliography

Ailes, R. *You Are the Message.* Ill.: Dow Jones-Irwin, 1988.

Bach, G. and Wyden, P. *The Intimate Enemy.* N.Y.: Avon, 1968.

Bird, J. *Talk That Sings: Therapy in a New Linguistic Key*, N.Z.: Edge Press, 2004.

Borysenko, M. *Minding the Body, Mending the Mind.* N.Y.: Bantam, 1997.

Buber, M. *I and Thou.* N.Y.: MacMillan, 1974.

Butler-Bowden T. *50 Self-Help Classics.* London: Nicholas Brealy, 2003.

Dyer, W. *Your Erroneous Zones.* N.Y.: Avon, 1995.

Elgin, O. *Promise Ahead.* N.Y.: Quill, Harper Collins, 2001.

Ellis, A. *A Guide to Rational Living.* No. Hollywood, CA: Wilshire, 1961.

Epstein, M. *Thoughts Without A Thinker.* N.Y.: Harper Collins, 1995

Fromm, E. *Escape From Freedom.* N.Y.: Henry Holt, 1995.

Fox, E. *The Sermon on the Mount.* N.Y. & London: Harper & Bros., 1938.

Gray, J. *Men Are from Mars, Women Are from Venus.* N.Y.: Harper Collins, 1992.

Grof, S. (Ed.) *Human Survival and Consciousness Evolution.* N.Y.: State University of New York, 1988.

Hendrix, H. *Getting The Love You Want.* N.Y.: Perennial Library, 1990.

Horn, S. *Tongue Fu!* N.Y.: St Martins, 1996.

Hubbard, B.M. *Consciousness Evolution.* Novato, CA: New World Library, 1998.

Jeffers, S. *Feel the Fear and Do It Anyway.* N.Y.: Fawcett Columbine, 1987.

Klein, A. *The Healing Power of Humor.* Los Angeles: Jeremy Tarcher, 1989.

Kornfield, J. *A Path With Heart.* N.Y.: Bantam Doubleday Dell, 1993.

Laborde, G. *Influencing With Integrity.* Palo Alto, CA: Syntony Pub., 1983.

Lewis, Hunter *A Question of Values* Crozet, VA: Axios Press, 2000.

Loeb, P.R. *Soul of a Citizen.* N.Y.: St Martins, 1999.

Maslow, A. *Toward a Psychology of Being.* N.Y.: John Wiley & Sons, 1998.

Maisel, Richard, Epston, David, & Borden, Ali *Biting The Hand That Starves You.* N.Y.: Norton, 2004

McGraw, P.C. *Self Matters.* N.Y.: Simon & Shuster, 2001.

Milgram, S. *Obedience to Authority.* N.Y.: Harpercollins, 1983.

Monk, G., Winslade, J., Crocket, K., & Epston, D. *Narrative Therapy in Practice*, N.Y.: Jossey-Bass, 1997.

Moore, Thomas *Care of the Soul,* N.Y.: Harper Collins, 1992.

Newman, M. & Berkowitz, B. *How To Be Your Own Best Friend*, N.Y.: Lark 1971.

Nierenberg, G. *The Art of Negotiating.* N.Y.: Cornerstone Library, 1968.

Nozick, R. *The Examined Life.* N.Y.: Simon & Shuster, 1989.

Omer, H. & Alon, N. *Constructing Therapeutic Narratives.* Northvale, N.J.: Jason Aronson, 1997.

Pearson, J. *Interpersonal Communication.* Glenview, Ill, : Scott Foresman, 1983.

Peck, M.S. *The Different Drum.* N.Y.: Simon & Shuster, 1987.

Pelley, J. *Laughter Works.* Fair Oaks, CA: Laughter Works Seminars, 1994.

Ray, P.H. & Anderson, S.R. *The Cultural Creatives.* N.Y.: Three Rivers Press, 2000.

Rogers, C. *On Personal Power.* N.Y.: Delacorte, 1977

Rosenberg, M.B. *Non-Violent Communication.* Encinitas CA: Puddle Dancer Press, 2000.

Seigel, Jerrold *The Idea of the Self,* N.Y., Cambridge University Press, 2005.

Sullivan, H. S. *The Interpersonal Theory of Psychiatry*, N.Y., Norton, 1953.

Tannen, D. *You Just Don't Understand.* N.Y.: William Morrow, 1990.

White, M. & Epston, D. *Narrative Means to Therapeutic Ends.* N.Y.: W.W. Norton 1990.

Wilbur, K, Engler, J., & Brown, D. *Transformations of Consciousness.* Boston, 1986.

Wilber, K. *Integral Psychology*, Boston: Shambala, 2000.

Acknowledgments

Many people aided me during the fifteen years in which I wrote and rewrote this book. I will mention only a few of the most recent: Dave Tilson, Frank Field, Michael Kaplan, Bruce Gourley, Lawrence and Suzanne Hess, Gerry Bailey, Gillian Hall, and my ever-loving wife, Nancy Hilyard.

Special thanks to my old friend Arnie Bernstein of New York City who gave me great help and support plus labeling this book "the ultimate self-help book."

Thanks to iUniverse who published this book and special thanks to their employees Agnes Hoepker, Rachel Krupicka, and the nameless editor that encouraged and inspired me to fully express what I wanted to express.

I hope that the many others who helped and encouraged me, and whom it would take pages to mention, know that I am very grateful.

978-0-595-36696-5
0-595-36696-1